# LET
# JUSTICE
# ROLL
# DOWN

# LET JUSTICE ROLL DOWN

## John M. Perkins

with Priscilla Perkins

BakerBooks

a division of Baker Publishing Group
Grand Rapids, Michigan

Published by Baker Books
a division of Baker Publishing Group
PO Box 6287, Grand Rapids, MI 49516-6287
www.bakerbooks.com

Printed in the United States of America

Library of Congress Cataloging-in-Publication Data
Names: Perkins, John, 1930- author. | Perkins, Priscilla, 1963- author.
Title: Let justice roll down / John M. Perkins with Priscilla Perkins.
Description: Young Reader's Edition | Grand Rapids, MI: Baker Books, a division of Baker Publishing Group, [2021] | Audience: Ages 9–12 | Audience: Grades 4–6 |
Identifiers: LCCN 2021009290 | ISBN 9781540901651 (casebound) | ISBN 9781540901415 (paperback) | ISBN 9781493431748 (ebook)
Subjects: LCSH: Perkins, John, 1930—Juvenile literature. | Voice of Calvary Ministries (U.S.)—Juvenile literature. | African American clergy—Biography—Juvenile literature. | African Americans—Mississippi—Biography—Juvenile literature. | Civil rights workers—Mississippi—Biography—Juvenile literature. | Christian biography—United States—Juvenile literature. | Civil rights movements—United States—History—20th century—Juvenile literature. | Mississippi—Race relations—Juvenile literature.
Classification: LCC BR1725.P47 A3 2021 | DDC 261.8092 [B] —dc23
LC record available at https://lccn.loc.gov/2021009290

21 22 23 24 25 26 27    7 6 5 4 3 2 1

This book contains graphic content
and parent discretion is advised.

Let **JUSTICE** roll down
like waters,
And **RIGHTEOUSNESS**
like an ever-flowing stream.

AMOS 5:24 RSV

# Contents

# Clyde

1

> **Sharecropping:** When a landowner allows a tenant (the sharecropper) to use some of his land in return for a share of the crops produced on the land.

Some things are hard to forget, maybe even impossible. The summer of 1946, after World War II, produced a horrible memory for me—one that haunts me even today. It was cotton-picking time again in New Hebron, Mississippi, when it happened. The summer heat was a scorcher, the steamy heat clinging like an unwanted blanket.

While whites owned some plantations in New Hebron, only a couple of them really had the money and resources of rich folks. The south-central Mississippi area was settled by whites after 1800. As customary in those days, whites used slaves to clear their property and plant crops. After slavery ended in 1865, landowners looked for sharecroppers to work their land, pick cotton for pennies a day, and pay back half their crops for rent.

Overall, whites in New Hebron were a heap better off than Blacks living there. But whites lived modestly enough that any change in circumstances was a personal threat to their livelihood. They needed to keep Blacks in line to maintain their lifestyles. Sometimes, they would resort to extreme measures to do it. For instance, while World War II was going on, a young Black soldier (a sergeant) returned home to New Hebron on furlough. He was in town one day, wearing his uniform, stripes and all. He was drinking heavily and boasting, too. Some white men decided the sergeant had too many big ideas. They grabbed him and beat him almost to death with an ax handle.

This kind of meanness upset Black folks, but we were helpless to do much about it. After all, the lives of our families were at stake, and that was more important than any thought of aggression. For some, the best way out was to leave Mississippi for good, head north or west, and never look back. Unfortunately, many Blacks hoping for a better life elsewhere found themselves in urban areas where they lacked the job skills to prosper. Their dreams being crushed, many Blacks from the South became the people who lived in deplorable conditions in the urban ghettos.

One person in our family had escaped life in Mississippi and seemed to be on the road to prosperity. That was my brother Clyde. The two of us were close, even though Clyde was twelve years older than me. Clyde had always stood up for himself, even before he got shipped off to Germany during the war—a war he did not choose to fight. During World War II, all-white draft committees discovered newfound authority to get "trouble-makin'" Blacks out of town. Clyde had been one of those singled out as a troublemaker because of an incident a few years earlier. He was a perfect candidate for the local draft committee to ship out.

That incident was an argument Clyde had with a white man. Disagreeing with a white man wasn't safe in those days, no matter how right you thought you were. My brother committed the unpardonable sin of challenging "The Man's" absolute rightness.

"I want to see you dead" were the white man's parting words to Clyde. It wasn't long before my brother was drafted into the US Army and sent overseas.

Clyde did pretty good in the army. He saw people and places he had never seen before and folks who accepted him just as he was. While fighting for America, he was wounded several times in Germany. We were just glad that he came home in one piece. He returned with an honorable discharge and a new attitude of confidence. Clyde was determined not to be pushed around anymore. He was a hero to all of us kids; we followed him around town, admiring his bravery.

On Saturday afternoons, everyone in New Hebron stopped working for the day, washed up, and went to town. They headed for Main Street to relax, window-shop, and catch up with people they hadn't seen all week. New Hebron's Main Street ran down a gentle slope from the dirt road at the upper edge of town to the railroad tracks at the lower end. From about two o'clock until nightfall, folks would be visiting with one another or just looking around. They came in cars and trucks, and some even brought their families in wagons pulled by mules.

Groups of Blacks—mostly sharecroppers and their families—drifted back and forth across Main Street or strolled along the sidewalks, wiping the sweat from their faces from time to time. Others sat around, fanning themselves and talking about the changes the far-off war had caused—changes that made a lot of people uncomfortable. This unspoken tension filled the hot, sticky Saturday afternoon air.

With so many Blacks in town, the white marshal was always there. He was on the lookout for trouble, even when things were quiet. The marshal walked along with the crowd, making sure everyone knew he was there. He looked straight into the faces of Blacks in each group, making sure no one was drunk or talking too loudly—reminding everyone who was boss in New Hebron. Blacks, especially the young adults and teens, had to weigh every word and action. It didn't take any particular reason for young Blacks to get in trouble. After eight thirty or so in the evening, it was understood that any Blacks standing around on the street were not welcome.

It was a Saturday evening when it happened (the memory I mentioned already).

Along about sundown, most farm families—both Blacks and whites—headed home. The parked cars and trucks would gradually disappear from the street. People who came by wagon went behind the stores to get their families on their wagons to head back home.

With the families cleared out, most stores began closing up. Most of Main Street grew quiet and still in the muggy heat. People who lived in town and others still around were mostly in the one-block area where a couple of cafes, drugstores, and Carolyn's Theater did business.

I was sixteen that September and visiting a friend's place near town, sitting around talking. Clyde was still on Main Street, out on a date with his girlfriend, Elma.

At the front of Carolyn's Theater, the big glass double doors welcomed whites to enter. To the left of the theater, between it and the five-and-dime store, a narrow alley led to a side door with its own ticket booth. Blacks used this entrance to go inside and up the stairs to the theater balcony to watch movies.

I didn't know firsthand but was told later that Clyde and Elma stood talking in the alley as they waited for the ticket booth to open so they could get movie tickets. People were getting restless, but Clyde and Elma stayed at the back of the crowd, still talking.

Nobody's sure just what started it all. Some folks say Clyde was talking loudly, maybe even arguing with Elma about something. A deputy marshal standing on the sidewalk yelled at them, "Quiet down."

Clyde had been facing away from the sidewalk where the marshal stood. As he turned to ask him a question, the officer clubbed him. Clyde got mad and, in self-defense, grabbed the marshal's club to keep the man from hitting him again.

Those who saw the whole thing said the marshal turned red in the face, so mad that he literally shook. Before anybody knew it, the officer of the law had taken two steps backward, pulled out a gun, and shot Clyde—twice—in the stomach.

As soon as the marshal left, a crowd of Blacks surrounded Clyde. One ran for a doctor. Others picked Clyde up—he was still conscious—and carried him across the street to Seay's Drugstore, where a doctor's office was in the back. Whites could walk in through the front; Blacks had to go around the building to the back door.

I was getting ready to get into a car with some friends when we saw another vehicle coming up fast, blowing a windstorm of dust in the air as it stopped. "Clyde's been shot," somebody yelled from the car.

My friends and I piled into another car and roared off toward Main Street. I didn't know the details yet, but I was sure somebody white had shot Clyde. That made me steaming mad! I wasn't the least bit afraid for myself. I was just fed up with all the things Black folks always had to go through. This time we ought to do something. We ought to get even.

A bunch of people were already crowded into the doctor's office at Seay's by the time we got there. I managed to push my way into the room, where Clyde was on the examining table. "The marshal shot him," Black folks whispered as I walked through.

Doctor Langston, the town's two lawmen, and one other white man were the only whites in that room full of Black faces and Black voices. That fourth white man was off to the side. I could see he was bringing in an extra gun and ammunition for the marshal. A heaviness in my stomach demanded relief. Right then, I would have shot that marshal if I had a gun.

Black faces watched the doctor, and then the marshal, their heads turning from the doctor to the lawman. The marshal watched all of us.

As more people jammed into the office, I went to the head of the examining table to be with Clyde. The doctor was leaning over him, working on his wounds. Standing at Clyde's head, I put my hand on his cheek again and again, mumbling, "Brother, don't die."

After a while, Dr. Langston looked up. "You have to get him to the hospital. I can't do anything more for him here." Jackson, the state capital and the location of the nearest hospital, was an hour and a half away!

We passed the word through the crowd, and soon my cousin Joe David had his '41 Chevy at the back door. Clyde was carefully placed in the back seat. Then my Uncle Bill and I got in, and two others got in the front seat with Joe. We rushed off into the night.

As the car sped toward Jackson, I could see life slowly slipping away from Clyde. He lay stretched out in the back, his head in my arms, oozing blood and dying by inches. How? Why? I kept asking myself questions, even though I knew the answers didn't matter much anymore.

No matter how things seemed, Clyde had to live. That was the most important thing now. All we could do was keep driving.

The miles to Jackson took us past the white folks' houses, the sharecroppers' shacks, the cotton fields, and the tall stands of pine against the black night.

At last, we reached the hospital in Jackson and got Clyde into a treatment room. All we could do then was wait. Other carloads of Blacks from New Hebron began to arrive. They waited, too.

I don't remember much else about that night. I do remember going into the room with Clyde for a few minutes. A white man was in the room. A doctor? Attendant? Someone waiting for a doctor? I don't know. Whoever he was, he just sat there.

Later, another white person came out to the waiting room with the word.

Clyde was dead.

Dead! My brother dead? All that fighting someplace in Europe didn't get him killed. He had come home safe from the war, only to be shot down six months later by a white man in his own hometown.

The anger I felt turned into a blur that had my mind in a tailspin. I don't remember leaving the hospital. I don't remember going home. I don't remember anything else until the funeral.

On the day of the funeral, Black folks came from all around, climbing to the hilltop four miles outside of town for the graveside ceremony. Truth is, my family wasn't known for being churchgoing people. So the man who said a few words at the graveside was the undertaker, not a preacher. It made no difference to me who said the words or what they said. I wasn't listening.

I saw the blue coffin laying open on the red clay earth. But the person inside didn't look like Clyde anymore. The undertaker's efforts had not kept the body from swelling and puffing.

The words were spoken and over. They closed the coffin and lowered it, and folks headed back to their homes.

It was over. There was nothing more to be said about it. There would be no official inquiry. If any whites stopped to think at all about my brother's death, they quite naturally took it for granted that whites in authority were always justified no matter what they did. No questions need ever be asked.

Black folks, too, joined in the silence. For some, the reason was clear: they knew where the power was. In the case of Clyde's death, he was dead, and Black folks were safer if nothing was said about it.

Other Blacks didn't say anything for another reason. When you've spent your whole life being told your place is at the bottom, the low image of yourself snuffs out any desire to get justice. The will to take charge of your life sort of dries up, like a muscle that never gets used.

Some Blacks were more like this than others. I'd go over to visit with a bunch of Black folks sitting around talking, and if someone mentioned the incident, there were usually some in the group who would just walk away. Clyde was dead. No need to talk about it anymore.

I stayed around New Hebron for several months before several relatives talked about getting some of our family out of town. Clyde was not the only family member likely to stand up to a white man.

The Perkins family was known as one of the toughest families around, with a reputation for gambling, fighting, and carrying on. A Perkins wouldn't take much off anybody, especially my Uncle Bill and Uncle Bud. They didn't care who they got into it with. Our reputation had a whole bunch of folks afraid of us—even some white folks.

My cooler-headed uncles in town were concerned that the younger kinfolk might act on their ill feelings about how Clyde had died. Somebody might do something against the white power structure.

So several family members left for California. I went up to Jackson for a while to live with my Aunt Lillie Mae David, who everybody called "Sister." She ran a rooming house for Blacks. Afraid for my safety, Sister and Uncle Bud got enough money together to put me on a train to head out West.

When I boarded the train from Jackson to New Orleans, I had one change of clothes, a lunch packed by Sister, and three dollars left after my ticket to California was bought. In New Orleans, I changed trains. The trip took me through Texas, New Mexico, and Arizona. The next stop was California. Mississippi was behind me.

*Forever*, I told myself.

The year was 1947.

# Jap

> **Plantation:** In the days of slavery, many wealthy landowners had huge farms called plantations. While slavery was legal, the landowners had their Black slaves plant crops, work the land, and bring in the harvest. After the practice of slavery ended by law in 1865, many free Black people in John Perkins's childhood continued to work on those plantation farms as sharecroppers.
>
> **Economic system:** A system of production, resource allocation, and exchange and distribution of goods and services in a society or a given geographic area.

he long train ride west to California gave me plenty of time to think—and to remember. Even at sixteen, a guy has a lot to remember. And a lot to forget.

I had no memory of my own momma. I was born in 1930, and my momma, Maggie, had pellagra. Her sickness kept her from being able to nurse me. Pellagra is a painful disease caused by protein deficiency. It was supposed to be a thing of the past in Mississippi by 1930, but Momma had it anyway. All she could do, I've been told, was lie there in that sharecropper's house by the cotton fields and try to get over it.

None of us knew at the time what protein deficiency was. We did know that milk helped. But nobody in our family (including relatives) owned a cow. The plantation owner said there wasn't enough pasture for keeping cows, so none of his sharecroppers could have one.

Because Momma couldn't eat or nurse me, I lay beside her, both of us growing weak from hunger. My grandmother found a sharecropper on a nearby plantation who had a cow, and that neighbor offered to give us some milk to feed me. Each day a little milk was brought over.

The milk helped keep me alive, but seven months after I was born, Momma died. Before I had any real consciousness of life, I had won my first battle with death. Looking back now, I know that God kept me alive for His work. It took many years before I thought much about God.

My father, Jap, left home around the same time that Momma died. Grandma—Jap's mother—took in all five of the Perkins kids—Clyde, Mary, Clifton, Emma Jean, and me. Grandma Perkins, "Aunt Babe Perkins" to everybody else, was a widow who had already raised thirteen of the nineteen children she birthed. Six of her children passed away either in infancy or childhood accidents. She took us in and made a home for us anyway.

Eventually, Aunt Babe gave away three of us Perkins kids. I was little, so she kept me. Clyde was big enough to help with chores, so she kept him, too. Aunt Babe lived on Mr. Fred Bush's plantation. And she stayed on his place for four or five years, from about the time I was three until I was seven years old. That's why my first memory is living with my grandma on the Bush place.

Mr. Fred Bush. I remember that name well. Learning and speaking his name at the right time would help me survive in a segregated society. In those days, my worth was considered only in relationship to a white man. If a Black child was walking along the road or was in town on a Saturday and he met an older white person, the white person's first words would be, "Whose place you live on, boy?" I had to know the answer. Who I or my family was didn't count. Sadly, I wasn't important in their eyes, but the person I was connected to was. My own name, John Perkins, had no significance. The name of the man who owned the land where I lived mattered. I had no dignity of my own. So right from the beginning, I learned to properly reply, "Mr. Bush's place, sir" whenever someone asked me where I belonged.

Our house on Mr. Bush's place had three rooms and a kitchen. A couple of aunts and uncles, some cousins, and I lived there. As many as twelve to fifteen people were in that tight space all the time. We managed, though. With just five beds in the house, the eight younger children (including me) slept in one corn-shuck bed—several at the head and the rest at the foot of the bed.

After a night's rest, we usually woke up to a breakfast of flour gravy, biscuits, and molasses. Grandma would heat up flour in a skillet with a dab of lard, stir the mixture until it was brown, and add water to make gravy. Sometimes she had a piece of pork or salt back to add to it. For lunch, we could look to having a piece of cornbread or some biscuits with homemade jelly.

Grandma's cabin stood on flat ground with the house backed against a stretch of woods of mostly pine and oak trees. From the front of the house, you could see cotton fields for most of the two miles to New Hebron.

Close by the house, a stream had cut a deep channel between the woods and the fields leading to Mr. Bush's house. The Illinois Central Railroad tracks bridged the stream at the place where we used to play and swim.

At noontime on days when the heat was blazing over the fields, we kids would bring the mules down to the stream to drink and rest in the shade of those tall oaks. We'd take advantage of the time to slosh around in the deep swimming hole or go play around the railroad trestle. I liked to climb up the slant of the braces, up onto the tracks, and back down again.

Growing up in the same house with a bunch of cousins could be fun sometimes. But other times, it hurt. Teasing, sometimes cruel teasing, was a regular part of our lives. My cousins had mothers who lived right there with them. I didn't. My momma was dead.

That's why one thing while living at the Bush's place comes to my mind again and again, exposing all the longings, fears, and emotions that caused me to continually reach for something more, something solid, something real—just for me.

The scene is the first memory of seeing my father, Jap. I don't know how old I was then, perhaps four. It is the first event that I can recall.

Even now, I struggle to explain just how important it was for me to see my daddy and to have him with me. My momma was dead. To not have a mother was painful, leaving me with a longing that eventually started me on the road to my life's work. Living in the Deep South during the Great Depression brought economic hardship and despair throughout the Black community. Life was tough. Families struggled for existence, yet somehow we kept going.

Teasing can be cruel, particularly if you are the only one without your father in the house. My father was not in the house, and I was open to all kinds of teasing. I had a father, and I knew it. My aunts and grandmother had told me so. I really wanted him with me.

One day, out of the blue, my daddy came home. He came up for a visit from where he lived in Columbia, Mississippi, and stayed with us overnight. He came late one Friday night after I'd fallen asleep. Daddy woke me up, and I saw him in the glow of the oil lamp. There was love in his face. Love for me. He hugged me in his strong arms. He talked to me. My daddy!

It's a wonder I slept at all that night. The joy of belonging, of being loved, was almost more than my heart could hold. I could hardly wait until morning to proudly show off my daddy to all those kids who had teased me. This was *my* daddy! I slept so good, knowing that his visit meant I would see a lot more of him.

I remember how I felt about having my daddy around more than about what actually happened the next morning. Daddy talked to me, showed special love for me. I almost didn't mind him calling me "Baby," since I was his youngest and all. I was so happy to be with him again—to see him and to touch him.

When he said he would be going into New Hebron with the regular Saturday afternoon crowd to catch a ride back to Columbia, my only thought was that I was going with him!

This was not a wish where you just choose something, like vanilla instead of chocolate ice cream. It was a deep-down feeling inside that we should, and would, go away together. After all, he was my daddy. My family!

Just after noontime on Saturday, Daddy started down the lane by the railroad tracks. I saw that he was heading toward town, and I followed him.

"Daddy!"

Jap turned and saw me following. "Go back."

The way he ordered me back sounded strange. But he didn't really sound like he was angry with me, so I followed. I wondered what was wrong. I knew my daddy loved me, so why didn't he want me to go with him?

As the lane ran out, Daddy moved up onto the railroad tracks. I trailed him. When he stopped, I stopped. When he moved on, I followed.

He knew I was still behind him because he came back and whupped me with a switch from a tree. After that, I stayed far enough back to run if he came toward me but close enough to see him through my tears.

I didn't know what to think. Why was Daddy punishing me? I hadn't done anything wrong. I only wanted to go with him. That's all I wanted, more than anything else in the world. Even when he switched me, I sensed that Daddy wasn't really mad at me. He just seemed worried.

My heart was breaking. Why couldn't Daddy see that I just wanted to go with him? I was terribly afraid that if he got out of sight, I would never see him again.

"Please, Daddy! Take me with you. Don't leave me alone again."

Jap stopped and looked back at me once more. That strange, sad look was still on his face. I wanted to run to him, but I was afraid. He still held that switch in his hand. I could only stand there and cry. I knew then that Daddy was going away without me. I still didn't turn back. So he came back and whupped me one last time.

I saw my auntie come up. She must have missed me and figured out where I was. I stood there between her and my daddy, but neither of them said anything. Auntie took me by the hand and dragged me away.

I looked back once, but Daddy was already gone. With him went my newfound joy in belonging, in being loved, in being somebody for just a little while. I cried all the way back to the house, holding tightly to Auntie with one hand and carrying my heart with the other.

What was Daddy thinking that day that he left me? I never found out. I never really had a chance to talk with Jap the few times I saw him again before he died.

But I do know that, even when he punished me that afternoon for following him, he was admitting that we had some sort of relationship. The need to have my daddy with me was a weight I carried, a need that remained unmet.

# Learning
# to Survive

**3**

> **Paternalistic:** Actions that limit a person or group from making their own decisions and living choices, supposedly for their own good. In this book, it describes whites who limited Black people's decisions about their own lives, as if the whites knew better.

The higher ground of the plantation beyond the stream led to the big house of Mr. Fred Bush. He had been a lawyer until he lost his hearing. But he was still young and could make a good life for himself here on the plantation. It was the sort of life in which, for a white man, hearing mattered less than talking.

The small cabins for house servants were close to Mr. Bush's house. The servants had been selected from among Blacks who were most agreeable to the ways of whites. For this reason, they were not always liked or trusted by other Blacks.

House servants didn't do sharecropping. The women of the two- or three-servant households on the plantation worked as cooks, maids, and nannies. Their men did the lifting chores too heavy for them and kept supplies of firewood on hand for the cooks. They also mended fences and tended to the buildings.

While all my family were sharecroppers until I left for California in 1947, the Bush place was the last big plantation where I lived. After my grandmother and aunts left the Fred Bush place, they always lived on smaller farms where their household was either the only one or the main sharecropping household on the property.

White attitudes made sharecropping the best option for most Blacks. As sharecroppers, we lived the proper role and behaved in the acceptable manner. Sharecroppers weren't considered dangerous people who would upset the system. Our family's status as sharecroppers gave us a stability of sorts that was not always available to independent Blacks.

Trying to be an independent Black in the postwar South could be risky. We might have been put out of business if we had tried to do that, running the risk of appearing "uppity."

Prejudice in the South was both paternalistic and antagonistic. What most Southern whites wanted was for Blacks to be part of the Southern system, to have a "proper" relationship with the superior white establishment. That's why independent Black farmers—small farm owners—had a hard time making it on their own without the help of whites, who had the resources.

In the system of paternalism, whites developed a feeling akin to ownership in their relationship with their sharecroppers/employees. This attitude was so strong that no one, not even a law officer who had business with a sharecropper, would go directly to him without the permission of the white landowner. Disturbing a sharecropper could be interpreted as disturbing his boss. Even as kids we learned to fear and despise the white man.

When I was only nine or ten years old, I heard that a young Black man accidentally ran over a white man. The Black was locked up in jail. Later, white folks came, took him out, tied him behind a car, and dragged him up and down the streets of that town that Saturday afternoon until he was dead. I remember it like it was yesterday, because that young Black man got killed just like my brother Clyde got killed: on a Saturday, on Main Street, by somebody white.

As Blacks so heavily dependent on the resources of whites, we found that cotton set the basic pattern of our lives because the whole community was all about cotton. I even used cotton planting and picking seasons to piece together my memories. When I tried to remember specific events that happened, I would say, "Well, we got in two crops at that one place, so we lived there two years," or "It was near the end of cotton-picking time when Clyde was killed." Strangely enough, this method worked for me.

Some things happened at certain times of the year. The cotton year began in January or February. Sharecroppers would go to the boss's house one at a time to make "arrangements" for planting and bringing in the crops. At that time of the year, the fields generally were dry and brown and the morning air crisp and a bit chilly. Only the pines were still green. When the sharecropper headed toward the boss's house, he might be walking in a hurry to stay warm, since the sun hadn't yet burned off the morning chill. Naturally, the sharecropper would go around to the back door to make his case for his estimated costs for planting and harvesting the cotton and other crops.

At the back door, the sharecropper would knock, and the landowner might invite him into the kitchen, the only part of a white man's house that Black field hands might get to see. Usually, though, the two men would talk outside.

After a proper "Good morning," the sharecropper might say, "Mr. Pierpont, I'm here to make arrangements for crops this year."

Mr. Pierpont would ask, "Okay, Bill, what are you going to need?" Or instead of using the worker's name, the boss man might use a favorite nickname: Red, Shorty, Slim, or whatever. A person without a nickname was uncommon in those days.

Sharecropper Bill might reply, "Ten dollars, sir."

Ten dollars a month was about the highest amount share-croppers were paid during the 1930s. Some smaller families might try to get by with less, although that would take a lot of extra work like hunting to keep food on the table.

Typically, Mr. Pierpont would scratch his head for a moment before replying. "Now, Bill, that's too much. You can get by on less than ten dollars."

Bill would keep at it. "But my wife had another baby."

The Man still wouldn't be convinced. "You can get by on nine."

After a few more minutes of this sort of talk, the men would agree on an amount and on the number of acres of corn and cotton to plant. With that being settled, another crop year would get underway. In those days, the sharecropper usually received half of the proceeds from the crops. The other half belonged to the landowner for rent.

The first task in February was to clear the land of dead brush and weeds. When I was nine, I had my own extra job for making money (about a penny each day). I fed chickens for a white woman who lived nearby. I'd do that early, then join Clyde, my cousins, and an uncle or two in clearing the land. The older folks did the heavy work, cutting with hoes and axes. We younger kids piled up the cuttings.

Before February was over, it was time to start breaking up the land. Boys as young as ten had to do their share of plow-ing. By the time I was old enough, Grandma Babe had died, and we lived with her daughter. My Aunt Coot lived only on small places, and my uncles handled all the plowing.

Plowing would go on through February, followed in early March by corn planting, and then planting cotton at the end of the month into early April. I'd be out every day putting fertilizer into the furrows by the handfuls or doing other child-sized jobs.

With the corn and cotton planting out of the way, we could do a little bit of planting for ourselves—peas and other veg-etables, watermelon, peanuts, and maybe a few other items. By doing this, we would have something to tide us over until the monthly arrangement with the boss could be settled. Share-croppers had to make it on their own from late summer until the cotton crop was harvested.

That's the way each year went. After we planted our vegetable patches, it would be time to thin out the corn. Next the corn would have to be chopped free of weeds. Then the corn would need one more round of fertilizer. Even though cotton was planted later than corn, it came up quickly, eight or ten days after planting. From then on, we were always picking cotton.

Peas sprouted up around May. Other vegetables came up later. We'd can some and eat some fresh. When I could, I'd go out berry picking with my cousins. But corn and cotton oc-cupied most of our time through the blazing hot summers.

Cotton harvest could last a long time. Some years, the first cotton wouldn't be ready until early August. Picking would continue in most places to the end of October or early November. Cotton-picking time was one time it was good to have a large family. Everyone pitched in. Field corn would be harvested well into November, and then another crop year was over. We sharecroppers would settle our accounts with the boss man and hope for a better crop the next year.

Not all Blacks picking cotton and corn were sharecroppers. Some—like those who owned small farms—picked cotton to earn extra money. After they'd get through picking their own crops, they'd hire themselves out as hands and pick cotton on other farms.

Those were days we'd all like to forget. But conditions in the cotton fields were still pretty much the same when I went west in 1947. A few years after that, plantation owners started putting big mechanized cotton pickers into the fields. A lot of folks were put out of work because of that. And since most Blacks couldn't get any poorer than they were and still survive, a lot of them migrated north. Those who stayed behind became almost destitute. Things still hadn't changed all that much for the poor in Mississippi. But change was coming.

# Challenging the System

**S**harecroppers lived from one crop year to the next, and only when the crop year ended did school begin. School couldn't interfere with farming. Since sharecroppers needed to be in the fields until all the crops were in, their kids didn't start school until late November or December.

Land clearing began in early February. That meant school for sharecroppers' children was about only three months a year: November, December, and January. With such a short school year, there was no such thing as finishing one grade in a year. It was more like finishing a grade every two years or so. For Blacks, our teachers usually came from outside the community for only the brief school year. An eighth-grade graduate could teach, but high school graduates were preferred.

During my first school year, I was still living with Grandma Babe, where I had first seen my father, Jap. We had never lived close to any school, so going to school didn't get much encouragement from family members. I don't remember anyone in our home ever getting excited about what school might do for me.

I was six years old when I started at Greenwood Elementary School. It was all Black, with all eight grades taught in the same room. On my first day of school, I ate breakfast with my cousins, wrapped up my lunch of biscuits and jam, and headed off with the group. When it was time to go home, I had a note from my teacher about the book I needed to buy. That was some kind of event for me.

My Aunt Ethel took me to the drugstore in town. She put down twenty cents on the counter, and I reached for that new thing that was mine. Now I could learn to read!

We had the usual three Rs in school—readin', writin', and 'rithmetic as they used to say. Sometimes a teacher would throw in an extra lesson on geography or health. But school health didn't have a whole lot to do with our health. I can still remember a teacher's solemn instructions on tooth brushing when no one I knew owned a toothbrush.

I loved basketball and baseball, two good reasons for going to school. Some of us boys made little carts with wheels we sawed off sweetgum logs. We'd climb on them and speed recklessly down the steep ravine behind the school. Getting banged up now and then only added to the thrill.

Since school was only in winter, I remember always being cold when I thought of school. We had wood-burning stoves in the middle of the room, but some days when it was too cold or if there wasn't enough wood, they'd just dismiss school. Firewood—like most everything else—had to be provided by the local community, since only teachers' salaries were paid by the county. Separate schools for Blacks and whites were the norm up into the late 1950s. Black schools, which had far less money than white schools, couldn't afford the luxury of school buses.

Every day on the highway near the Black section of town, big, beautiful yellow school buses whizzed by, taking white students to their schools. Black students walked to school, often dodging spitballs thrown from the windows of the buses that passed them.

Few rural Black Mississippians made it to high school during that time. Black high school students not fortunate enough to live near a high school for Blacks often had to find room and board miles away from home during the week.

I think I reached about the fifth grade before I finally quit school for good. It didn't matter much to my family anyway. No one encouraged me to go to school or church.

My reasoning for quitting school was that I already was learning my most important lessons in life outside the classroom. In fact, I was only about eleven or twelve when I got my first lesson in economics. I didn't learn it in school; I learned it on the job.

That hard lesson happened when I was away from home, visiting a friend of mine. I agreed to help a white man from a plantation in the area get his hay inside quickly before it rained. This man needed somebody to help him haul hay, and I needed some money. I figured maybe I could work all day and make a dollar and a half or two dollars. That was what a day's work was worth at that time, and that's what I expected to get.

I went to work for that man, and I worked all day. At sundown, he handed me fifteen cents. I could hardly believe it. Fifteen cents!

Here I was, standing in the white man's kitchen after doing a man-sized job for him. Fighting against anger and disappointment, I didn't know whether to take the dime and buffalo nickel. I was afraid if I accepted the money, I would hate myself for taking it. I was also afraid that if I didn't take the money, the man would say I was uppity. At that time in Mississippi, it was tough enough just being Black; to be known as uppity would have been unbearable if the word got out. And it would.

Twelve years old. My first time going out on my own in the workday world. My first encounter with a white employer was also my first encounter with "the system." Feeling defeated, I took the fifteen cents.

As I left the man's house, I took a long look at what had happened. This difficult first lesson began my pursuit to understand economics. The white man had the capital: the land and the hay. He had the means of production: the wagon and the horses. All I had were my wants and needs—and my labor.

I had been exploited. I told myself, *This system is a system based on capital. Get capital, control it, and know how to use it. To make money in this society, you have to gain the means of production. Then, you will have the choice of doing good or evil with it.* This man had done evil with it. He had exploited me. From that day on, I began to understand the economic system and how it works.

By the time I was thirteen, I saw myself as a man. I made a lot of my own decisions. I felt comfortable thinking for myself, which was something I got from my grandmother, a strong-willed woman who was intelligent and self-confident. Grandma Babe had no fear at all of white people.

So I guess it wasn't much of a shock when my first challenge to the system happened when I was fourteen. My cousin Jimmy went with me in search of making some extra cash aside from the chores I had at home. We contracted to cut some heavy bushes and undergrowth from a pasture owned by a white farmer. Most people thought of this man as fair-minded. He had the reputation of always giving those who worked for him a good meal. Jimmy and I agreed to work for a gallon of syrup and a meal per day.

This was tough work, requiring us to work hard and steady all morning. At lunchtime, we went around to the kitchen for our food. The farmer's mother-in-law met us at the back door. Instead of giving us the meal we had agreed upon, she handed us meat trimmings and scraps from their table. Then, she closed the door.

Jimmy and I looked at our plates and then at each other. Who could work all day on a handful of leftovers? We decided we couldn't and wouldn't. We went home, leaving the job and the tools.

When the farmer—the lady's son-in-law—heard what we did, he got upset and came over to our place. He asked us to come back and finish the job and promised that we could eat at his mother's house, which was not far away. We agreed and went back to work. That incident always stuck in my mind. It was my first small push for justice through economic pressure.

I became more and more independent and eventually took my first trip away from home. I had heard that my father was still living in Columbia. I headed south to visit him. When I got there, I saw that Jap's girlfriend didn't like me at all. That didn't stop me from wanting to stay as long as I could with my daddy.

Aunt Coot soon found a job for me and persuaded me to return to New Hebron. I went home and took the job. I hated it; I really did. I had done small cash jobs for whites before, but this was the first time that I worked for a monthly salary under the direct supervision of whites. My work had mostly been sharecropping with my own family. What we always did was our own concern, our own project.

This time was different. I worked for the Smiths, a white family of unmarried sisters and a brother who lived in one

of the few old antebellum homes in our area built before the
Civil War. The pay was twenty dollars a month. I felt I should
be getting more. But even if I got more money, I didn't want
to keep working there. I promised Aunt Coot that I would,
but deep inside I knew I couldn't stay on much longer at the
Smith place.

I didn't know it then, but a bigger change was in store for
me—much bigger than just another job. It was late summer,
1946—only a few weeks before my brother Clyde was killed.

It would be only a few months before I headed west to
California.

# Who Needs Religion?

Ninety-eight cents an hour. That's what I got in 1947 at my first job in California at the Union Pacific Foundry in South Gate. Forty dollars a week was good money. I could still taste the bitterness of that twenty dollars a month back in Mississippi.

Money was only part of the good feeling I had. In Mississippi, every move I made was defined by my race. I worked on farms and fields, behaved in certain ways toward my employers, and received certain wages—all defined by my blackness.

In every one of these areas, the standards were different for whites.

In California, I got the same wages as whites and worked right alongside them. Over the years, I've learned that racism exists nationwide. But at that time in Southern California, I could see glimpses of hope for a much better future.

Clyde was dead, and so were the old times back in Mississippi. I was not going to look back. I pushed on with my new life. I was staying with a cousin in the town of Monrovia. We drove sixty miles or so round trip together every day between Monrovia and South Gate.

At the foundry, I was part of a crew making cast-iron pipes for sewage and plumbing. Production was going strong. Workers voted to join the United Steelworkers union. Because I had already done a good job helping to organize the production line and managing men, too, I became our department's union steward.

As production increased, pay remained at the same hourly rate. The workers felt we deserved a bigger piece of the action. After all, we had helped devise the system that was bringing in that extra profit.

I got right in the thick of organizing a strike that brought our workers a number of new benefits, including a provision in which we sometimes earned one hundred dollars a week— good money for those days. I never forgot the power of united action.

I was not yet out of my teens when all of that happened.

In 1949, I went back to Mississippi for a visit. That's when I met Vera Mae Buckley again. I say again because relatives say we played together as kids. Neither of us remembers that.

Vera Mae's first recollection of seeing me was at my sister's funeral when I was real young. My sister had been killed by her boyfriend. Vera Mae remembered how sad it was when she got home after the funeral. She asked her grandmother, "Who was that little boy standing under the tree crying in the middle of the graveyard?"

"Oh, that was Tupy, one of the Perkins boys," her grandmother had told her, using the nickname my family gave me. Vera Mae's grandmother went on to tell her more about the Perkins family.

Vera Mae was raised by her paternal grandmother, Brillie Williams. Her family had a good background and was among the few small farm owners in the area. The Williamses went to church regularly, making them just a bit suspicious of that rowdy, not-church-going Perkins crowd. Church folks, you see, had lots of rules. No smokin'. No drinkin'. No cussin'. My family did all of that. Her family wasn't too sure a Perkins offspring would be good enough for one of their girls. When I began courting Vera Mae, her family just didn't know what plans God had in store for both of us.

Vera Mae and I met one Sunday on the church grounds. And the way we met tells a lot about what the Black church was like in the 1930s and '40s. In those days, church was where Blacks could go for a social life. Church folks didn't go to the movies. Few people owned cars, and even fewer could just drive to Jackson when they wanted. In those days, the church was where young folks met their future spouses.

Ever since slavery, the Black church in the South has served as one of the few places Black people could get together and speak freely. At church revivals, people came from all over town. At larger gatherings like church association meetings, people from churches all over the county and surrounding parts came. The atmosphere was festive, with booths set up to sell every kind of food, chewing gum, and candy late into the evening. Fish sandwiches were a specialty. The women filled big pots with hog fat and formed an assembly line. They would cut big buffalo fish into slabs, fry them in the fat, and make sandwiches.

These meetings at church were among the most acceptable ways of socializing in those days. Some people came to church not necessarily to worship but to eat, court, and socialize. These special meetings continued in the South until about the early 1950s, when thousands of Blacks moved north for better jobs. With more cars, mobility became easier, and the social value of the meetings became less important.

During the height of the social meetings at church, men sat on one side of the church and women on the other. The young people sat on the center pews. When the preacher ended his sermon, deacons got up and announced, "It's time to take the offering." The congregation began singing. Then starting from the back pews, the people stood, marched to the front, laid their money on a table, and went back to their seats. Most of the men and boys went outside to socialize. When the offering had been taken and church dismissed, the girls came out.

On this particular Sunday, I was already outside, standing around on the Pleasant Hill Baptist Church grounds, when Vera Mae came strolling out of the church. Like a lot of the young folks, I was there for socializing, not for worship. I didn't know a lot about God at that time, and it would be a few more years before He became a priority in my life.

Vera Mae came outside, and I got real interested. She never noticed me, but I saw her. I liked what I saw. She was the most beautiful Black woman I had ever seen. She went and got into a car with a girlfriend and sat there talking.

I walked over to the car and began talking with Vera Mae. She seemed glad to see me. I was more than glad, because I knew I had met the girl I wanted to marry. "Vera Mae, you're going to be my wife someday," I said to her. Just like that.

If Vera Mae was surprised by my sudden proposal, she didn't act like it or say anything. She didn't say no either.

While my family wasn't known for being churchgoers, the real reason I wasn't religious is that, in all my years growing up in Mississippi, I had never heard the central message of the gospel, the good news of great joy for all people—that Jesus Christ could set me free and live His life in me.

Yes, I'd been to religious services as a kid, of course, but I never learned that I could have the power of God in my life, a power that could make a difference in me and in my surroundings. The few times I'd been in church, I had watched everybody get emotional. I couldn't see how all that shouting I saw in Black churches was giving people any kind of incentive to develop. I also didn't see that life was any better for them than it was for me.

In fact, I had always viewed Black Christians as inferior, somewhat ignorant people whose religion made them gullible and submissive. Religion had made so many of my people humble down to the white-dominated system with all its injustices. Religion had made them cowards, I had rationalized.

I was a Perkins. I wasn't like that at all. No way was I like that. I did not see how Black Christianity was relevant to me and my needs. I did not see white Christianity as meaningful either. For me, Christianity was part of the whole system that helped to dehumanize and destroy Black people.

In the South, I drank from separate water fountains, rode in the back of buses, and suffered other insults made legal by Jim Crow laws. Never in the South had I heard one white Christian speak out against the way whites treated Blacks as second-class citizens. I had never accepted the lie that I was a second-class citizen. I did not see the white Church as relevant to me and my needs.

When I got back to California, something happened that changed my thinking and my life.

# A Patch of Blue Sky

After meeting Vera Mae, I went back to California. We wrote letters back and forth until we met again in 1951. I was sure happy to see her. And after having read all those letters from me, Vera Mae was glad we could meet face-to-face once more.

We had good times together and began making plans to get married. The Korean War came along, and our plans were put on hold because I got drafted.

Later that same year, 1951, I got a twenty-one-day furlough after finishing my basic training. Vera Mae and I decided to get married. By the time she got ready, got packed, and got out to California on the train, seven days of my furlough were already gone. But we got married anyway and had somewhat of a whirlwind honeymoon in the few days we had left.

Just two weeks after we were married, Vera Mae returned to her family in Mississippi. I went back to camp and was shipped overseas to Okinawa, Japan. Right away, I missed her a whole lot.

Vera Mae was the closest link to Christianity that I had ever had. In all that time—in my new job and through my whole time in the army—I had no genuine Christian contact, no one who really understood the gospel and the Christian life. My mind was seeking, but due to my background, my motivation was mostly political and economic.

Beginning in 1951 while I was in the army, I started reading and gathering everything I could find from troop information centers and the library. I began to understand why the United States was in the Korean War. By this time, President Harry Truman had issued an executive order mandating integration of the US military at all levels. Being in the armed services allowed me to interact daily with whites and various other ethnicities with every sort of personal and political view. This was a defining moment in time, preparing me for the community-building work God would later have me do.

In the army, I saw firsthand how other people viewed money and how they related themselves to the economics of their daily lives.

I was not a drinking man, even in the places I was stationed, where liquor was readily available. The practical effects of my lifestyle—no drinking and simple living—meant I had extra money. For the first time in my life, I could turn the tables on the white man. I could loan him money, at interest, remembering the example set by the white landowner who charged us sharecroppers interest.

As sharecroppers, Blacks had no choice. The kind of borrowing we did was out of necessity for our very lives. But in the army, white men borrowed money simply because they couldn't handle themselves and their appetites.

After two years in the army, I was discharged and went straight back to my cousin's house in Monrovia, California.

Vera Mae was still living in Mississippi. I thought at first about going to Mississippi to bring her back with me. Going back would give me a chance to see my father again, too.

I knew my father was sick. Jap had had a heart attack and had been staying at Aunt Coot's place ever since. Aunt Coot was sort of our family center and main communicator; her letters had kept me updated about the family while I was in the army.

Vera Mae came to Monrovia soon after I got there, saving me a trip back to Mississippi. She brought fresh word about my father. He was getting better, everybody said. Since he seemed to be out of danger and Vera Mae was in California, I decided I would stay in Monrovia.

Just a few weeks later, Aunt Coot called to say my father had died. I flew back to New Hebron the next day to bury him. When I got there, I found a mixture of joy and sadness. The family was really glad to see me again after all that time away. But my coming home could not take away their sorrow about another death in the family.

It was winter when I went to Aunt Coot's ramshackle house with its old fireplace. You see, before a country funeral, the tradition was for people to come to the home of the deceased. Every visitor who knew the dead person would sit down and listen to a relative tell the details of how the person died.

So Aunt Coot sat me down and began to talk. Only in my case, she started the details of what happened a bit further back because I had been away so long. I was different now and had moved on to new things. But so much that was still a part of me seemed to settle down in that room as we talked of years ago and the people who were part of my life.

At one point, Aunt Coot turned toward me and said, "Jap had hoped you would come home when you got out of the service,

Tupy. He'd only been sick for about a week then, and he was getting better, but he was hoping you'd come home. He'd been wishing for that."

That caused me to be very sad and was a wonderment of sorts to me. It was hard for me to believe. My father had wanted me. He really had! Yet I had never known. I was so uncertain of how he felt about me that I had just stayed on in California, looking for a job. I didn't come home in time. But I didn't know that he cared.

Daddy's funeral was at Oak Ridge Church, a nice brick church. One of my cousins preached the funeral. I stood there a long, long time under that February sky, just looking down and thinking.

I tried to bury my memories, too, by going back to California as soon as possible to make a good life for Vera Mae and me. It wasn't that we were full of bitterness, because we weren't. California was a place where we could forget all the bitterness—a new land offering a new life. We tried to forget the bad memories from down home in Mississippi.

I threw myself into the thing I considered most important—a good job and good money. I was determined not to accept just any old job but one that had opportunities for me to move up. All my life, I had lived with an invisible ceiling above me that said, "You're Black, and you can't go no higher." I was used to hard work; I wasn't looking for an easy job. I just wanted one with a patch of blue sky above me instead of that ceiling.

I started as a janitor with the Shopping Bag Food Store Company. A couple years later, I explained to the company president that I wanted to keep working there but I needed to move up. He offered me a job in the welding shop, where I learned welding. I showed them I could learn machinery—any machinery—quickly. Better than that, I drew on my earlier union organizing experience and showed them I could supervise people, too. I started moving up.

By the spring of 1957, I felt I had pretty good chances in life. That good feeling was not just about the money I was able to earn. I was a provider for my family. I was a man.

I was going places!

# God for a Black Man

I had a lot of questions about life that I couldn't answer. I spent a good bit of time just wondering, and I was beginning to ask questions about religion. This led me to question the value of religious beliefs, including those of Muslims, the Jehovah's Witnesses, cults, and others. For a long time, I didn't recognize this searching as being religious.

It was impossible for me to imagine that the white Church, the private club of the oppressors, had anything to do with reality and justice. I also examined the merits of communism and capitalism.

Prejudice, of course, knows no boundaries. It can be found anywhere. But at that time in my life, I hadn't developed a total hatred for all whites. You see, in California, I was finally getting somewhere and getting there with the help of white employers.

Those feelings that I had back then were mostly directed against the South. I couldn't see any peaceful way to change the South. So I was convinced that someday there would be a Black uprising south of the Mason-Dixon line. I was anxious for that day to come.

But God stepped in. Those years in California gave Vera Mae and me a unique time to be developed and prepared by God without the pressure of hatred and malice toward the South. It also gave us exposure to a world much bigger than the one we grew up in.

I was with a good company and moving right up. Vera Mae was a trained cosmetologist, fixing hair and planning to have her own shop soon. We had good friends and a nice house. We were making it in life. We were bringing up our kids in a better atmosphere than we had ever known as kids ourselves. Our children and family became the center of our lives. While I was shy and had a problem with stuttering, I still made a lot of friends.

Something was missing, though. Vera Mae and I both needed something deeper and greater in life. Vera Mae kept going to church but only haphazardly, and I went with her to Second Baptist Church, Monrovia.

I began to see God work in "mysterious ways" during the spring of 1957. He did it quietly, first through our oldest son, Spencer, and then through a good friend at work, Calvin Bourne.

Spencer was going to a children's Bible class at a little church down the street from where we lived. He was happy going there, and we didn't mind anything that made Spencer happy.

In those days, we never said a blessing at the table; we just ate. But after he started going to the children's Bible class, Spencer started saying verses at home before we began to eat.

I watched our son. I could see something developing in him that was beautiful, something I didn't know much about. I had no real experience seeing Christianity at work like that in a person's life, in a good way.

Spencer kept after me to go with him to his Bible class. Because I loved him so much, I finally agreed to go. His life had become so radiant I wanted to find out what the Bible class was all about. I found they were teaching the Bible.

Calvin, meanwhile, had been inviting me for years to go to his church, the Bethlehem Church of Christ Holiness in Pasadena. He finally convinced me to start going with him.

It was the first time we hit upon some zealous Christians who had genuine love and concern for people. The older mothers of the church were just like parents to us. They took us under their wing, even inviting us over regularly for Sunday dinner.

At Bethlehem Church of Christ Holiness, I got to know Rev. Matthew Richardson, the pastor, and his assistant, Rev. James Howard, who also was a Sunday school teacher. These Black men told me how they had found "new meaning in life through Christ." Their words had a ring to them. I was curious because this was all new to me. I was always interested in new ideas. So I agreed to join an adult Bible study class taught by Rev. Howard on the book of Acts.

I was twenty-seven years old then, but this was my first encounter with the Bible as a book of truth and value for my life. Prior to this, I had viewed the Bible as a book full of make-believe and old wives' tales. Why would any intelligent person bother to read it? Only religious people did that. I had always thought of religious folks as being inferior people who could not make it in society.

Once I make up my mind to do something, I do it. I was a good student. The Bible became my motivation, strength, and enlightenment. I tackled it with fervor, grasping the precious insight within its pages through April, May, and right on into summer. I enjoyed reading it. Every day I studied my Bible, carefully working my way through the New Testament. Every week I met with the study group, joined in the discussions, and asked questions, mostly about Paul.

The thing that really hit me about Paul was the motivation he had. By this time in life, I was super-motivated myself, but I was motivated for my own economic betterment. As I read and studied the life of Paul, I saw that he was super-motivated, too. But his motivation was unselfish. His was a religious motivation.

That got to me. How could religion mean so much to anyone? Paul had drive and determination. And he had even more enthusiasm. But what was it that made him tick? I had to find out.

To help me in my studies about Paul, Vera Mae went to a bookstore in Monrovia and bought me a commentary on the book of Acts. Mary Feastal, who ran that bookstore, would later become a very good friend. Even back then, the Lord was already at work weaving our lives together with others for His own purpose.

Meanwhile, summer became fall, bringing more study, more work, more questions, and more discussions. I learned that Paul endured so much for religion. Why? I still didn't see anything in religion that would cause a man to want to give up his life and endure all that Paul suffered. As I looked at religion, it was not something to suffer for; it was something to suffer with.

One night at home, the Spirit of God for the first time took the Word of God and spoke to me. I was reading from Galatians 2:20 where Paul says, "I am crucified with Christ: nevertheless I live; yet not I, but Christ liveth in me: and the life which I now live in the flesh I live by the faith of the Son of God, who loved me, and gave himself for me" (KJV).

I'd never heard about Christ living His life through me.

I realized I didn't have that life. It was a defining moment when I found authentic faith. The kind of life Paul was talking about came from total yielding to Christ—the opposite of my self-pushing. My motivation and my hope didn't produce the kind of contentment Paul had. I studied hard, and because I now knew more about the Bible, the Christians in our church apparently thought I was a Christian. But I knew I wasn't. Paul told me that.

The following Sunday, I went back to our Sunday School. Vera Mae was home, pregnant with Derek, so I went to church alone. That morning, the pastor preached a sermon on Romans 6:23: "For the wages of sin is death; but the gift of God is eternal life through Jesus Christ our Lord" (KJV).

That verse of Scripture spoke to my whole experience. It hit me hard, and the Holy Spirit began to speak to my heart.

Wages. Pay. From my experience, wages were what I got as a young boy, when I was old enough to work hard but young enough that a white employer could excuse himself from paying his Black laborer a decent wage.

Yes, I sure did know about wages. But—wages of sin? What was this preacher talking about?

I thought I knew about the "wages of sin." Union organizers had talked to me at the foundry about stopping exploitation. All my boyhood experiences taught me what that word meant. Exploitation was sin.

But was there other sin? My sin? Back and forth from life to Scripture my mind went that morning.

For the first time I understood that my sin was not necessarily and altogether against myself or against my neighbor. My sin was against a holy God who loved me, who had already paid for my sins. I was sinning in the face of His love.

I didn't want to sin anymore. I wanted to give my life to Christ so that He could take care of my sin. I sensed the beginning of a whole new life, a life that could fill the emptiness I had even on payday.

God for a Black man? Yes, God for a Black man! This Black man! Me!

That morning I said yes to Jesus Christ.

# Winners and Losers

**8**

I had peace like I'd never felt before.

After church, I went home and told Vera Mae what had happened to me. Calvin Bourne came over, too, all happy and excited. "The brother got saved this morning," he said enthusiastically.

I was genuinely saved that Sunday morning, and it led me and the whole family to really dedicate our lives to the Lord.

I moved into my new life like I did everything else—as hard as I could. I began sharing Christ with people in the area where I lived. Those church members who thought I was already a Christian could now see some real changes in me.

True Christian change works more like an old oak tree in the spring, when the new life inside pushes off the old dead leaves that still hang on. That's how God worked in me.

I began reading everything about Christianity that I could get my hands on. I had so much to learn. I kept going back and forth to the bookstore where Vera Mae had bought the commentary for me. Mary Feastal did more than sell me books. She prayed for me, and she worked with me on my speech,

helping me with pronunciation and teaching me how to practice speaking without stuttering. My speech began to improve.

Vera Mae and I became involved in Child Evangelism
Fellowship, sharing Jesus with little children. Vera Mae had
been saved through Child Evangelism as a young girl, but this
Christian teaching was brand new to me. When I examined
it closely, though, I saw the same thing that I had been taught
in the adult Bible class that had helped bring me to God: an
emphasis on learning, on getting something solid.

Vera Mae and I both began teaching classes among the
Black children of Monrovia each afternoon at five o'clock. We
also attended the leadership training workshops every Tuesday night. We both were passionate about anything we felt
strongly enough to get involved in, and we gave it everything
we had.

In those workshops, I found something I never expected.
In addition to Bible learning, I met white Christians. It's hard
to describe how odd, how different that whole experience was
for me. These were not just white church members, but white
Christians—white people who said that God had actually
changed their lives.

Every Tuesday night, I sat with my white teacher, Mr. Wayne
Leitch. God was taking me step by step. First, God showed me
Black people changed by the gospel. Now He was showing me
that it had power even for whites.

Mr. Leitch didn't hold me back with any rigid ideas of what
he thought my abilities would be. When he saw what I could
handle, he offered to work with me during afternoons, too. My
job by this time was in El Monte, where he lived; so I would
stop by his school at three thirty every day after work to learn,
think, and talk man to man, Christian to Christian. We met
together like this for the next two years.

Along with working, studying, and teaching, I began to do lay preaching at Sunday night services, sharing my testimony at white and Black churches. I didn't do very well at first. Being asked to preach the sermon at our church on New Year's Eve was a good example of my early efforts to deliver a solid message. Just before I was to start, Calvin Bourne discovered that he'd forgotten something for our communion service. So he dashed out to the store.

After he left, I got up to preach on "A Voice Crying in the Wilderness." I went through my outline. I guess it only took me about thirty seconds. That seemed kinda short, so I went through it again. Then a third time. Having nothing more to say, I sat down.

About that time, Calvin came puffing back and thought he hadn't missed a thing. The rest of the service went on for a while, and finally he leaned over and whispered to me, "Hey, Brother, aren't you gonna preach tonight?"

"I did already," I said.

Calvin's still wondering about that one.

From the spring of 1958 until 1960, people in the surrounding cities really got to know me. Many of those residents became my friends for life. I look back at my experiences in the area and all that happened to me the next two years as preparation for my return to Mississippi. Seven years after I got back to Mississippi, I was asked to serve on the board of directors of World Vision International, the largest mission relief and Christian development organization in the world. In that role, God gave me insight about the depth of hurt in the world and how His Word can heal even the most desperate situations, including those where hope seems impossible.

The dignity of knowing Christ was reflected in the love the people in that valley had for me. It was a period during which

God taught me about true love. I held Child Evangelism classes nearly every afternoon of the week. I seemed to be more effective with boys, since they were the majority of the students in my class. But that was not what kept me teaching. Being able to tell the salvation story brought me great joy, and sharing it with these young folks made it all the better.

Other Black Christians helped me see the need for person-to-person adult evangelism. Four of them—Rev. Curry Brown, Rev. George Moore, Mrs. Elizabeth Wilson, and Mr. Jim Winston—joined me in gathering an informal group that would later be called the Fisherman's Gospel Crusade. We knew that Blacks around Monrovia needed to be confronted with the real Christ, the Christ for them. Churches, of course, also needed to be preaching this doctrine, but there still was a great need for the whole gospel to be communicated person to person. So we began a simple program.

Each Sunday afternoon, we met on Mrs. Wilson's porch. Then we'd decide, if we didn't already have an invitation, which family we would visit that afternoon to share our faith. In this ministry, we learned to depend on each other. It was a group effort. In the home we were visiting, one or two people would share a personal testimony, and they would generally have me make comments about certain passages of Scripture. Then we all joined in the conversation.

Many Blacks in the area, if they had any contact with churches, were used to just listening to sermons. Others simply ignored religion, the same as I had done. But we gave everyone a chance to actually have some input about the Bible in relation to their own lives, allowing them to ask their own questions and to find answers in Scripture for themselves.

We weren't trying to form a new church group. We were simply determined to allow our own faith to make a difference for Christ in the community where we lived. People who found new life in Christ through this house evangelism joined local churches, so churches often gave us the names of friends or relatives to visit. At other times, we might get an invitation directly from a wife or husband to come talk with their family or to a roomful of people.

All this activity kept me busy, but I still looked for other opportunities to share my faith. One of these would change the direction of my whole life. It came when a bookstore owner put me in touch with the Christian Businessmen's Committee of Arcadia-Monrovia. I had an opportunity to mingle with a group that was at the time an all-white group. For a while, I was the only Black member. There, I met John McGill, who later became one of my best friends. He was on the board of Child Evangelism Fellowship.

I really got involved with these Christian businessmen. Soon they were asking me to share my testimony here and there. I was also teaching Bible classes every night. After a while I found myself constantly on the go. You know, every Sunday morning, every Sunday night, through the week— some place, some church, some group. I got so busy I didn't have time anymore to look at the system around me. I almost forgot my upbringing.

Two of the Christian businessmen I knew, Ed Anthony and Dean Saum, asked me to go with them to visit California prison camps in the San Bernardino Mountains. The boys in these camps were only thirteen to seventeen years old. They helped take care of the fire outbreaks occurring in the mountain areas.

I soon found out why my friends asked me to go with them. A majority of the prison population in these camps was Black. A Black witness to Christ was needed. And that witness was me.

We held Sunday morning Bible classes for the young men at the camps. Each time we went, I shared a brief testimony and spoke from the Scriptures. The young prisoners were often suspicious of me. Some of them came to the meetings simply because they were bored and had nothing else to do. But I began to see young men's lives change.

One of the first times I spoke, there were thirty to forty young men listening. I poured all my effort into that sermon. When I was finished, two of them came down to ask Christ to change their lives. They were crying.

But it wasn't the response or the emotion that affected me most. It was the stories of their lives that started me wondering about my real values and goals as a Christian.

These young fellows were on their way to being real losers in society. In their minds, I was what I looked like—somebody who had made it. To them, this businessman-preacher was just another visitor from that other world, the world of winners. And they were losers.

They didn't know my background, but I knew what I was and what I had been. From that point forward, I began to ask myself more and more what special responsibility God had for me. The boys in the prison camp often had backgrounds just like mine. Their voices and their accents sounded like guys I grew up with. Some of them had come right from the same Deep South I had known, or they were the sons of Blacks who had fled that closed society. Like me, they came without skills or education. Like me, they didn't have a strong religious background. Like me, they had dreams of "making it" in California. But a funny thing happened on their way to success: it's called failure.

I couldn't figure out all the reasons I ended up with a future different from theirs. God had now made me one of His own, but I didn't feel that I had survived because of any personal goodness on my part.

I had more than survived. God had let me succeed where these young men had failed. I had a good job, good opportunities. My wife had a good job, too. And here these young men were in jail, in trouble. Yet God loved them no less than He loved me.

So if God had done all this for me, and if He loved them as much as He loved me, what did all this mean? What did it say about my plans for my "good" Christian life?

First, I saw more clearly that the root of many of the Black man's problems lies in the unsolved problems of the South I had left. I couldn't escape a conviction growing inside of me that God wanted me back in Mississippi to identify with my people there and to help them break the cycle of despair—not by encouraging them to leave but by showing them new life right where they were.

Soon the conviction became a command. I remember the night God spoke to me through His Word about going back to Mississippi and starting a ministry for Him there. I was giving my testimony to an all-white church in Arcadia, California. Standing before the crowd of people gathered, I used as my text Romans 10:1–2, where Paul says, "Brethren, my heart's desire and prayer to God for Israel is, that they might be saved. For I bear them record that they have a zeal of God, but not according to knowledge" (KJV).

God took the power of Paul's love for His people and shot it through me, saying, "John, my desire for you is that you go back to Mississippi, because I bear your people witness that they have a zeal for God, but it is not enlightened."

I was reminded of the emotionalism of many of the Mississippi congregations I had seen and heard. I recalled the fact that most Black preachers pastored four or five churches at the same time and had little or no opportunity for real Bible training.

God was calling me.

I was never again satisfied in California.

# A Hard Command

**W**hen I started sharing my vision of a Mississippi ministry with friends, some told me that I should forget about it. After all, I had a wife and a growing family. I could be a Christian witness right where I was.

The friends I had made in the Fisherman's Gospel Crusade were sad. We had become a good team, but they would not stand in God's way. So they pledged monthly support and their prayers.

I spoke with the pastors of two white churches—Calvary Bible Church in Burbank and Arcadia Union Church. Both pledged to help through monthly support and their prayers.

Vera Mae had been so happy when I accepted Christ, but she didn't count on it taking us back to Mississippi. We had been living in Monrovia on our rising income, able to move from our little house on Pomona Street into a big, twelve-room, two-and-a-half-bath house on Los Angeles Street.

The idea of returning to Mississippi didn't sit well with Vera Mae at first. I knew God was calling me to go back because I felt the call. Vera Mae didn't. The more I talked about going back to our home state, the more she resisted the idea.

On top of that, I got sick and lost a lot of weight. I became so weak I could hardly stand.

Vera Mae took me to the Long Beach Veterans' Hospital many times. The first diagnosis was ulcers. The ulcers healed, but I kept losing weight until I had lost more than forty pounds. Doctors checked my heart and other vital organs, but everything seemed to be okay.

I talked about quitting my job. Vera Mae reminded me that we had "all these young'uns to feed." Besides, we also were expecting our fifth child, Deborah. I kept going to work, but my health issues did not go away. I became so weak in November 1959 that I couldn't stand. I couldn't even get out of bed.

I didn't know it then, but the Lord had been speaking to Vera Mae, too. He was telling her that she had to let me go, or she might not have me at all.

She admitted later that the Lord had shown her that unless she gave in to His calling on my life, she would not have a husband. "Either I yielded, or I would lose you, Toop," she told me. The thought of "having to raise five children alone was a frightening thought," Vera Mae said.

One morning, Vera Mae came into our bedroom and knelt by our bed where I was lying awake. She said, "Toop, I'm going to pray for you."

She prayed aloud, so God and I could hear her: "Lord, it's a hard struggle for me to say yes, but I'm going to say yes. I'm willing to go. I don't want to go, but I'm willing. Lord, I'm saying yes to You."

Then Vera Mae prayed some more, asking the Lord to raise me up again and use me any way He wanted. When she finished praying, her burden was gone. The great choking feeling in her heart was gone. That prayer of surrender gave her peace with God about His purpose for my life.

Vera Mae's peace made me feel better, too. I felt God raising up my body and my spirit.

The next day, which was a few days before Thanksgiving, I was up and walking around. I felt well enough to tell Vera Mae, "I'm going to Mississippi to check things out." She was okay with that now. The day I left to go south, Vera Mae and the kids—Spencer, Joanie, Phillip, and Derek—took me to the little bus station in Monrovia.

I had to make that trip. We all knew it. Before I left, we stood in the bus depot, holding tightly to one another. Vera Mae and I sensed that this little trial separation was just the beginning, that it was just a taste of some of the bigger trials in our future.

I didn't want to leave my family in Monrovia. We all knew we'd be lonely. As believers, we knew that yielding to God's will was our only option.

By Thanksgiving, I was back in Mississippi but without a detailed strategy for going forward. I knew I needed to pave the way for moving the family to Mississippi with me. In my old hometown of New Hebron, I spoke in a few churches and talked with people as I tried to figure out where and how to work most effectively in what God had called me to do.

The disturbing images of those broken Black lives in the California youth detention camps continued to haunt me. I knew our greatest potential for reaching young lives was while they were still reachable. Child evangelism seemed to be the answer. I was convinced there was a ministry for us among the youth of Mississippi.

I stayed six weeks in the state, scouting the territory. On Christmas Eve, I called Vera Mae. "Honey, it's me, Tupy! Can you come on down and pick me up?"

"Sure, Toop, where are you?"

"I'm right here in Monrovia at the bus station. I just got back."

I heard happiness in Vera Mae's voice. I could tell she was glad to have me safely home again. Thanksgiving had been lonely, but Christmas would be different.

By June, our house in California was rented, freeing us to live again in Mississippi. On top of that, we had a little money in the bank. We loaded up a U-Haul trailer and hitched it to our '56 Chevy on June 6. By June 9, we were back in the same Mississippi I had once left "for good."

# Under the Skin

**Emancipation:** President Abraham Lincoln issued the Emancipation Proclamation in 1863 to free enslaved people from bondage in the Southern states, making them "thenceforward and forever free." The realization of "forever free" continues to be questioned today.

Back in Mississippi, Vera Mae, the children, and I went to live with her grandmother near New Hebron. We were back in the same old world I had left. The same area where Clyde had been killed. The same place I had left—for good. Here I was back in the state, not because Mississippi had changed but because God had changed me and called me back. Almost from the word go, my ministry became our ministry—a family ministry. God had called us back to Mississippi as a family.

During the rest of the summer of 1960, Vera Mae and I organized some vacation Bible schools. The short Bible schools were new to these people. There were churches for Black folks all around, but the religion they got there was not for learning; it was for getting emotional and for socializing. I wanted to catch their hearts with the truth that had caught my heart—that the Bible was for learning about God.

The children didn't know me personally, but I knew their world, their language, and I had their brown skin. In one location, our vacation Bible school started with 10 children on the first day. At the end of two weeks, we had more than 120, including a number of adults. More opportunities for witness in the Black schools came that fall.

You can't really understand my experiences or the experiences of Black children in Mississippi unless you know a little bit of the history of education in the state. Many changes have come, especially since the late 1950s when Mississippi was forced to revamp its school system. While made reluctantly under the growing threat of federal pressure, most changes were for the better. But that didn't necessarily mean a change of attitude by white society.

Even before changes were made, it was understood that if schools for Black children had to depend on public tax funds alone, they would never have existed. Many Black schools in Mississippi existed because of private effort more than public taxes. Missions and various private organizations provided people and money for Black education. Tougaloo College, Mary Holmes College, and other schools were established and funded by northern white Christians. Private organizations contributed tuition aid, teacher training, teachers' salaries, books, and school buildings. Local Black communities without the financial resources to help did their part by doing such things as supplying labor to raise buildings and maintain them.

Julius Rosenwald, chairman of Sears, Roebuck & Company, set up a huge fund of several million dollars to help. He did not donate school buildings outright. His grants had conditions attached to stimulate local efforts. In the Black community, "local effort" almost always meant the churches because they were the strongest social organizations in the local communities. Because of this, the growth of Black schools in Mississippi before the late '50s was often the result of partnerships with churches. In fact, some schools were built right beside churches, making them overlapping institutions in those communities.

On May 17, 1954, in *Brown v. Board of Education of Topeka*, the US Supreme Court ruled that "separate but equal" schools were not equal and were, thereby, unconstitutional. You can't add up in dollars and cents all the injustices of the old "separate but equal" educational system, but following the money trail can give you a pretty good idea.

In the year before that famous *Brown v. Board of Education* court decision, official Mississippi Department of Education figures show that the state had 544,405 students registered in public schools, divided almost evenly between Black and white children. While the number of children involved was basically equal, the extent of unequal distribution of money for their public education was hard to deny:

| TRANSPORTATION | | INSTRUCTION | |
|---|---|---|---|
| White: | $4,476,753 | White: | $23,536,022 |
| Black: | $1,179,826 | Black: | $8,816,670 |

These wildly different expenditures were done according to "proper" procedure. State educational funds were granted based on the number of total students in a county. But then, separate budgets were made up, using different minimum standards for Black and white schools. Since each Black student "required" less money for his education than a white student "required," it turned out that those counties with the highest percentage of Black students actually had the best schools for whites. More money was available due to the larger number of Black students, but most of the money went to fund the education of the smaller group of white students.

Of course, part of the problem was that Mississippi has always been among the poorer states as far as income goes. So naturally it has had less money overall for everything, including education. There never seemed to be enough money to provide everybody a good education.

Any suggestion that whites were exploiters was out of the question. Even whites sometimes felt that their children were not getting an adequate amount of money for education. Sadly, those whites who got only the minimum eighth-grade education still got it at the expense of Blacks. Their education helped them get the right jobs and make their way in the world.

Obviously, this unequal system so firmly entrenched in the thinking of white Mississippians would lead whites to respond negatively to the 1954 Supreme Court decision declaring the inequity of "separate but equal" education in the state. This negative response of whites to the decision was strong, even hysterical. Governor Hugh White stood up tall and reassured everyone that Mississippi was "never going to have integration in its schools." For quite a while, it seemed possible that the state would go so far as to close down the entire public school system just to avoid integrating it.

The schools didn't close down. Compromises were made that "unified" the previous separate school districts on paper. Segregation continued by administratively assigning pupils to various schools in the new districts.

The state hoped for sympathy by sharply increasing expenditures for Black schools. School buildings went up everywhere—brick buildings in every county, it seemed. Every county got school buses. Visible changes took place all over the state, replacing the old one- or two-room schools with full-scale buildings. These changes also would require more Black teachers.

When I got back to Mississippi in 1960, the stress of movement and change was stirring in the air. There was so much to be done and so much to fear in the atmosphere of poverty, illiteracy, and rigid segregationist feelings ingrained in the culture. But interest in the new schools and the focus on education change helped boost my first project—child evangelism.

That fall, when I went to register my children for school, I listened to the orientation session held in the church next door. The principal seemed to be under extraordinary pressure to prove himself acceptable to the community, so he was careful to show himself as a good community man. This was the opportunity I needed. It would be hard for this man to turn down my offer to enrich the school program.

After the orientation session, I introduced myself to the principal. "How about some Bible classes for the students in your school?" I asked.

"Fine," he said.

I smiled inside and began preparing right away to teach Bible classes in the school at New Hymn near Pinola. We did well there, and our newfound reputation helped open doors in other schools.

I also became involved at Prentiss Institute, a Black junior college. The founders, Mr. and Mrs. J. E. Johnson, had been students of George Washington Carver and Booker T. Washington. Mr. Johnson had died, but Mrs. Johnson was still active at Prentiss. For years she had felt a need for a spiritual emphasis at the college, although she wasn't sure how to do it.

She invited me to speak at a Religious Emphasis Week at Prentiss. Somewhere around forty kids accepted Christ. On the final night, the new converts gave their testimony to the whole group at the meeting. After that, I became the regular chaplain at Prentiss Junior College, continuing my other work as well.

The Bible classes at Prentiss, as with all my work, were taught with the assumption that Christianity is a fellowship of believers, not just a collection of individuals.

As a Bible teacher and pastor, I didn't lean simply on my skills in classroom teaching. It was just as important for me to let people know I was also concerned about their daily needs. Our income, lifestyle, needs, and problems matched a lot of the concerns of these people. We could live among them as friends helping friends instead of well-off outsiders with no understanding of their issues and concerns.

After finding a house in Mendenhall, the county seat of Simpson County, we were able to move out of Vera Mae's grandmother's house. Most of Mendenhall spread over a long slope, with the main business street stretching down from the courthouse at the top. Farther down, across the railroad tracks, across the highway, along some narrow and winding streets, was the Black section of town. It reminded me a little of my hometown of New Hebron.

Our house was just down the street from a two-story cinder-block building once used as a dormitory for Black high school students. For three years, until she finished high school, Vera Mae was one of the students in that dorm, going home on weekends.

We lived in a tiny rental house in Mendenhall, and later rented a small storefront just down the street that gave me some office space and storage for supplies as well as space for Bible club meetings.

The next year, we bought a large tent for holding meetings. These were not your usual "tent meetings" with flashy singers and a big production and all. No way. We had preaching, but there was more emphasis on teaching and Bible classes than anything else.

People showed up for the tent meetings, which were set up in each place for at least two weeks. We got to know them, and we made a lot of headway using the tent ministry for a couple of years.

The same year, in 1962, something big began in a very small way. I knew we would have to get our own property sometime instead of continuing to rent. So I took the money in my savings account and, for less than $900, I bought five small lots on the outer edge of the Black section of Mendenhall. The street was not paved. Trucks bringing supplies had to unload on the paved surface not too far away if they came during rainy weather. We contracted with a builder to put up the shell of a large house. Using the labor of teenage boys I'd been working with, we finished the interior ourselves.

I knew that if the gospel was ever going to change the hearts and lives of the people, I needed to preach a *holistic* gospel that they could embrace. A gospel of hope, love, and justice. That meant developing fellow coworkers and not just Bible club students.

This new house was big enough to hold the weekly youth meetings in the large downstairs living room. I knew that God had already blessed our ministry in the lives of young people, but it was still a nice feeling to have this new building as a physical sign of our hope for Mendenhall.

# It's Nice to Have Friends

As our work grew, money became crucial. Late in 1963, I knew I needed to reach out to some of my contacts in California for more support to meet our next big need: a school building.

I headed for California envisioning a better life, this time in Mississippi. My goal was $3,000 for bricks and other materials for the Bible institute building. Milder weather in Mississippi made construction costs a bit less than elsewhere.

I had a lot of experience working with people but not in fundraising. In my prayers, I was conscious of the human barriers I faced and the need to trust God for this project's success. He would have to multiply the few contacts I had without fancy brochures, movies, or slides of our work. All I could do was open myself up to those who would listen and tell them about the needs in Mississippi.

Calvary Bible Church of Burbank, California, pastored by Dr. Jack MacArthur, was an important stop. This church was interested in rural ministries, and I became one of their rural ministry representatives. The church also sponsored a radio broadcast called "Voice of Calvary." It seemed natural, under the church's sponsorship, to call our own ministry Voice of Calvary as soon as the next building went up.

The pledges came in. Counting that money, along with some of my own that was left over after selling our house in California, I returned to Mississippi with $6,000—twice the goal I had set. We had enough money to buy a secondhand bus and began working on a brick ministry building next door to our house.

It wasn't long before we found ourselves organizing a church, although that wasn't part of our original plan. In 1964, we formed a new congregation, the Berean Bible Church.

While the church was growing, I was invited to speak in Dallas at a school where Artis Fletcher, the first kid I discipled in Mendenhall, now attended. Businessman Kirk Lamb heard our story and gave us enough money for yet another building, which we would use for a chapel. We used some of the money to buy the adjacent land, where we would later build a gymnasium.

I worked with two white men to organize some Bible classes. Rev. Kenneth Noyes, a mission worker, and Rev. James Spencer, a Presbyterian minister, became my first white coworkers in Mississippi. This partnership didn't last long. In the 1960s, the Ku Klux Klan, and people who claimed to speak for them, was still active. The civil rights movement had resurrected the visible acts of hatred of this old racist organization. Rev. Spencer had roots in the local area, making him more vulnerable to threats against his family and his career. Hateful phone calls in the middle of the night would awaken him. I could see he was feeling the strain. Finally, it was too much for him to bear. He decided to leave us.

We were able to add other courses to our Bible classes when a highly respected Black teacher, Mrs. Annie Bell Harper, began teaching English and speech for us. Mendenhall's Black school was founded by her and her husband and named in their honor. Harper School kept that name until court-ordered integration in the '70s brought in white students and made it a junior high school. Naturally, the all-white school board and the white parents could not tolerate their children attending a school named after a Black person. The school was renamed Mendenhall Junior High School.

The heart of our work was to grow a community of young people and faithful older Christians right in Mendenhall. With the help of Vera Mae and other colaborers, I kept up the Black public school ministry that began the summer I got back to Mississippi.

The youngsters in the school ministry were starved for real Christian guidance. This ministry appealed to young people because of our talks, flannelgraph stories, and songs. We also offered free New Testaments to anyone who wanted one. We could usually find churches and mission groups willing to give us Bibles. Finding financial support to attack hunger and economic despair was not as easy. But it was good that we could always get Bibles.

Here and there, I caught glimpses of white Christians trying to weigh the value of the time-honored ideas they had accepted from their upbringing. One local white minister in particular, Dr. Robert Odenwald, pastored First Baptist Church of Mendenhall. At first, he was a bit cold toward me and the work of Voice of Calvary. Not hostile, just cold. Since I had some business matters to talk over with him about one of our community projects, I made up my mind to get to know him. Perhaps we could establish some common ground between us.

I went uptown one day to see Dr. Odenwald. Black men—even Black ministers of the gospel—didn't visit white ministers of the gospel. But Dr. Odenwald had shown some interest in our work. I told him what I was doing and why I believed God had called me to my work. I explained that we had a Christian ministry in Mendenhall trying to reach young people for Christ, letting him know some of the areas we went into and the people we met—areas and people who were part of a different world from his.

I didn't ask Dr. Odenwald for support. I hadn't come for that. Our conversation began to drift to our faith. I discovered that he was interested in whether I was a real, Bible-preaching Christian. He didn't know how to label me. I told him that I shared his faith in Christ alone, that Ephesians 2:8–9—saved by grace alone—was my message, too.

We had a long conversation, looking beneath each other's skin color to discover the things we had in common. As we talked, he became radiant, maybe even excited, to know we were preaching the same gospel.

Dr. Odenwald showed me a book he was reading, which was the true story of a Black preacher named John Jasper from the days of emancipation. Jasper was one of the most famous Black preachers of that time, and even whites came to hear him preach. For years he could preach only on his days off from the tobacco factory where he worked, but he finally ended up with his very own church.

Jasper's boss, after hearing about his conversion and preaching, didn't discourage him. He told him, "Preach the Word, John, preach the Word." And there in his study, the white minister I was speaking to turned to me and told me, "Preach the Word, John, preach the Word."

Then the two of us prayed together—right there in his office. As I left, the man was crying. I had never seen a white man so moved. I thanked God for showing me Himself at work.

Dr. Odenwald and I had more conversations over the next few months. I wasn't bothered when I learned that whites were beginning to notice our friendship. The Spirit of God was at work.

On the other hand, it was a real struggle for Dr. Odenwald, who like so many others was hindered by tradition. He tried to express something of God's love for *all* people in a couple of sermons and even voiced the contradiction he saw between his own biblical convictions and the social attitudes of white society that he and his congregation accepted without question. Cautiously, he tried to preach the real meaning of Christian love as it applies to the sin of racism.

His effort was met with absolute resistance. In fact, some whites didn't see any connection at all between their minister's new sermons and the Bible. They only saw that the pastor was acting strange.

I could tell that Dr. Odenwald was under great emotional stress. I did not know or understand the extent of the stress he faced until it was too late. One night, while I was driving with the radio on, I heard that he had committed suicide! I wept in my heart for this man who had tried so hard to build a bridge of understanding between his people and ours, the same kind of bridge we had built so slowly and so carefully between the two of us. I had hoped Dr. Odenwald and I would have the opportunity to link our two communities together.

"Why, God?" I asked. "Why?"

I went to Dr. Odenwald's funeral. The casket was closed. I was the only Black at the service, but that was okay. White funerals are a little different from other white events. In the days of plantations, when the white plantation owner died, all the Black folks were asked to come because it would be nice to say that the man was loved by both Blacks and whites. It's too bad that death is the only time when some people think of that—love, I mean.

The next time I took my clothes to the cleaners after Dr. Odenwald's death, I said to the owner of the business, who had been a member of his church, "It's very sad about Dr. Odenwald."

"Yes," she said, "it is." She went on. "The last few Sundays, he'd been acting strange. He was talking about love and concern, but in a sad way."

*Was it really that strange to hear all that talk about love and concern?*

*Are love and concern really as rare as that? So sad,* I thought.

# The Whole Gospel

From 1965 through 1967, activities of the civil rights movement were going strong—sometimes in the wrong direction. Malcolm X was shot and killed. Riots erupted, and both whites and Blacks were killed. Action and reaction kept growing and spreading. Chicago, Dayton, San Francisco, and Watts were hotspots.

In word and action, Blacks declared, "We are human!" We realized more strongly than whites that the time had come to stand up for the same privileges and opportunities as they had. Laws were passed, but they often were dismissed as un-constitutional. Round and round, attempts were made to twist *equal* and *freedom* into neat packages that would allow whites to continue to enjoy the privileges they had.

I talked with a lot of people at the many civil rights ral-lies I attended. I was an evangelical Christian, and our Voice of Calvary Bible Institute was growing. Our young people in Bible school and college were gaining a political, economic, and spiritual awareness of how the world worked.

By going to those rallies, I could tell that trouble was brew-ing. Rioting and burning were symptoms of valid issues being raised in and by groups that were not primarily evangelical.

The great contribution made by the civil rights movement to the Black man's struggle for justice and equality is undeni-able. Those who led the movement were committed men and women, committed both to the cause and to the struggle.

It's sad that so few people professing Jesus Christ ever be-came a part of that movement, one that was political in nature but sadly lacking the spiritual input needed for balance.

The vast majority of Bible-believing Christians ignored the civil rights movement altogether, missing out on a great and crucial opportunity in history for ethical action. The evan-gelical church, whose basic theology was the same as mine, was among the church leadership that stayed on the sidelines. The major principles of the evangelical church are founded upon the belief that salvation is through Jesus alone and that believers must share this good news of salvation with others. I decided to act, placing myself squarely between the two: the church and the civil rights movement. I knew, of course, that we wouldn't get anywhere unless we started with the gospel, calling men and women to Christ for forgiveness and God's strength. Man cannot create justice by human manipulation, nor can the church use "spiritual" manipulation to create justice.

In California, when I was first saved, I got busy right away, starting Bible studies, training classes, child evangelism programs, and other activities. I wasn't shutting out society's ills. I suddenly saw how much there was to do and to learn.

In 1965, civil rights issues were heating up. Everyone—Blacks and whites—had to take a stand. I was more than an evangelist. I was involved with a growing institution and needed to stand up and be counted, too. At the same time, I was still responsible for our Bible institute and for young people trying to get into colleges. There were other responsibilities as well.

By the time of the civil rights movement, we at Voice of Calvary were working with people of all ages. Vera Mae started a childcare center in 1964. In 1966, with additional funding, the center became a Head Start program.

As a result of seeing so many family problems, I started teaching several teen Bible classes. I wanted to make sure that these kids didn't get just some isolated "religion." I wanted them to learn solid principles for family life. Vera Mae and I were the first generation of the Perkins family since slavery to actually stay together as a family. Our children, and the children we worked with, needed a model for building their own healthy families—something I never had.

The youngsters came to know that we operated under the principle that every young person needs to know who he or she is and why they matter. With their own families someday, they would have to make up their own minds and act accordingly about politics, economics, and other issues around them.

Besides the children and the teenagers, adults were getting involved as well. They took Bible classes. They also provided support for the young people's activities.

I could see that the outcome of integration efforts to provide an equal education for Black students certainly would bring a lot of new money and help to Black communities. Unfortunately, most white churches were silent about this important issue.

Two hundred years of slavery, followed by two or three generations of economic exploitation, political oppression, racial discrimination, and educational deprivation had created feelings of inferiority, instability, and dependency in the Black community. Lacking a sense of self-worth or self-identity, far too many Blacks turned to self-destructive behaviors.

The gospel of Jesus Christ, with its power to transform people by the renewing of their minds (see Rom. 12:2), is so important to the Black community. It has the power to heal and restore self-worth.

At the same time, as I observed the white evangelical church community, I saw that white folks, who I had come to identify with in religious faith, were going to have to deal with me in the area of social concerns, too. I couldn't abandon those concerns, nor dismiss them.

What I saw was not entirely a "Black problem." White people, too, have failed to allow the gospel to speak fully to them, to lead them to address exploitative and unjust lifestyles and behavioral patterns. If Christ is Savior, He also must be Lord over areas such as spending, racial attitudes, and business dealings. The gospel must be allowed to penetrate the consciousness of both Blacks and whites.

That might seem cut-and-dried, but things are never as simple as we think. I found that out in a hurry. Many Blacks had adjusted to the Southern way of life and weren't interested in rocking the boat by pushing for political or economic equality.

As Voice of Calvary began voter education and got involved in voter registration work, a number of Blacks began pulling away from us, seemingly because any effort expecting them to stand on their own was frightening. It was almost like they still lived in the old plantation days of slavery. These "don't rock the boat" Black Christians looked down on the rest of the Black community, an attitude that kept them from sharing the gospel of Jesus Christ with the Black community they claimed to be so concerned about.

Whites did not reject my natural hairdo and beard as often as these evangelical Blacks who had made their peace with the status quo. So I shaved off my beard. But voter education and voter registration were nonnegotiable activities that had to go on.

I prayed for more Christians with real biblical convictions to come help with voter registration and such and to be a testimony to the bigness of the Bible—how it is a guide for the life of the whole person, addressing an individual's personal and social actions.

Each year, I visited the churches in California that supported our work. I found that some of my Black evangelical friends there also had a measure of personal satisfaction and economic opportunity in their lives. As in Mississippi, they weren't interested in problems of inequality and injustice outside their personal circles. I talked to them about other Blacks trapped in a closed system quite different from theirs. But they were afraid of getting involved. Still, I talked to them about a lot of things—including voter registration.

Inequities are inevitable when the political, social, economic, and legal institutions are dominated by whites. Voter registration was just one way that Blacks hoped to participate in those institutions controlling their lives. Whites in the South were so used to running things that even the efforts to get Blacks registered to vote appeared to be dangerous radicalism. I told my California friends about my home county, Simpson County, where only fifty Blacks were registered to vote before voter registration efforts began. In a registration drive one summer, we got more than a thousand Blacks registered and ended up with more than twenty-three hundred.

The chance to live a whole, full life in the South was very important to those of us living in the South. People outside southern boundaries sometimes viewed our activities with suspicion. Some of my white supporters thought I was using my time and their money for something different from their idea of religious activity. Their concerns would be expressed in comments like "The whole idea of you going back there was to get people saved. Don't you think you are getting away from that?"

Salvation, of course, was the foundation, goal, and everything in between of our efforts. But what did the Bible mean by "brothers in Christ"?

I wanted to share what Christ had been doing for me. Surely it wasn't God who was incomplete here. Maybe evangelical Christians, Black and white, were confusing theology with the status quo.

At times, it seemed that God was being packaged and handed out by people who had used the Bible in a way that would benefit their best interests. It seemed to me that some of the institutions claiming to help Blacks actually contributed to the cycle of dependency and poverty. A Bible school founded and run by white Southerners was able to get other Southerners to help train the "poor, pitiful Black people for the gospel" but was not at all interested in anything that would challenge the status quo. They didn't offer a genuine solution that would move Blacks forward. They didn't even admit we had a problem.

Some of our support began to dry up. In speaking engagements at both Black and white churches, I tried to defuse some of the standard objections, oftentimes seeing them coming before questions were raised. For instance, someone might ask, "What do you think of Martin Luther King Jr.?" I knew exactly where that question was leading. So I would say, "You know, I lived in Mississippi. I grew up in Mississippi. I used to ride on those segregated buses—sitting in the back of the bus. That's dehumanizing. When I went to a restaurant, I had to go around back in all those dark, dirty places. That hurt. I saw people with hardly enough to eat, and I knew many who were killed—not because they had done anything wrong but just because they were Black."

I would tell them things like that, things they knew were still going on. They had to admit that these things were bad. We didn't usually get around to discussing King because they could guess that I would probably ask, "What are you doing to help correct these bad things?"

Usually the question would be sidestepped to something like "But you don't agree with violence, do you?" My reply would be something like this: "I don't believe that, overall, Black folks believe in violence. Most Black folks have been living in a state of violence in Mississippi and the South under conditions of white supremacy and segregation. Yet I don't know of one Black person in Mississippi who has killed whites because of the situation."

Then I would remind them: "Violence, in relation to civil rights activities, is a reaction of whites to Black people who want nothing more than their freedom."

While that soaked in, I would keep talking.

"In my activities, in my work, I don't even consider the question of violence. I'm not thinking on that level at all. I think on the basic level of freedom.

"Of course, there are some Blacks who have gotten a lot of newspaper coverage because of violence. As a Christian, I believe that all men are sinners, and that includes Blacks capable of turning against their fellow man.

"But in the overall history of Black-white relations, it's a different story. The worst violence is the violence against Blacks, the kind that usually is so accepted within the white system that it gets no publicity at all. The fact is, there are many more whites who believe in violence or who believe in ignoring it when whites do it. But the Black person always gets asked about violence."

I said what I felt needed to be said, just stating facts as I saw them. I never severed ties, never cut off communication with anyone willing to talk. Love is a giant thing if the person who has the complaint will not break the relationship.

I kept seeing new things that needed to be done. Waking up the middle-class evangelical church to its responsibilities was one of them. Some evangelicals did not argue directly with me. They merely felt uncomfortable with me and hoped I would disappear without them having to suggest it.

During the years 1965 through 1967 my personal battle was not with what I believed. I knew that the Bible commands us to seek justice. I had already thought that through and had come to firm conclusions about it.

There were, and always will be, human emotions. I felt sadness at seeing those I knew as brothers in Christ insist on a religion that didn't sharpen their sense of justice during those years of turmoil. The justice of Jesus was something I couldn't hide. It wasn't a question of what "team" to join. When it came to social justice, evangelicals didn't even have a team on the field.

Sadness came from other directions, too. I watched ardent civil rights activists object to social inequities without bringing God into the picture. Still, I decided that if something was right, I would do it as a command from God—not because some non-Christians also thought it was right.

But I kept longing for the day when Christians would take seriously the words of the prophet Amos:

> Take away from me the noise of your songs;
>     to the melody of your harps I will not listen.
> But let justice roll down like waters,
>     and righteousness like an ever-flowing stream.
>     (Amos 5:23–24 RSV)

A discouraging example of religious charity happened in the fall of 1966. That's when my children Spencer and Joanie joined six others in becoming the first Black students in Mendenhall's previously all-white public high school. At the same time, an evangelistic effort through the school chapel program caused many white young people to make a public profession of faith. But walking down the aisle in a religious meeting to announce a new life in Christ apparently did not persuade anyone to step across an aisle at school to greet or get to know even one Black student.

For two years, Spencer and Joanie walked through lonely halls where no white person would sit down with them. No white student ever held a conversation with them. And no student, teacher, or adult religious leader in the white community admitted that anything was wrong with the situation.

I had to watch. It hurt. I kept asking myself, *Does the gospel— that is, the gospel as we presently preach it—have the power to deal with racial attitudes?* If evangelism is truly on the side of God and His love, then it should never allow itself to look like it's on the side of a bigot-producing system.

After two years of that stressful environment, we sent Spencer and Joanie to California for one semester. When they returned home, Spencer was enrolled in the Black high school and Joanie at Piney Woods, a private Black school nearby.

In 1970, a comprehensive integration program was mandated by court order in Mendenhall.

# Taking a Stand

Thanks to the "ingenuity" of the Mississippi Plan, the percentage of Blacks in Mississippi eligible to vote for president in 1964 was dismal compared to the numbers who voted in the 1896 election of William McKinley for US president.

The Mississippi Plan, proposed in the state's 1890 constitution and adopted the same year by the Mississippi Constitutional Convention, voided the political gains Blacks won through the Fourteenth and Fifteenth Amendments to the US Constitution and the Civil Rights Act of 1870.

With the new state constitution legalizing the Mississippi Plan, and stronger legislation securing it in place, whites restored "time-honored customs" that again stripped Blacks of even the most basic rights.

The Mississippi Plan outlined requirements for voting, being careful not to mention Negroes (Blacks) specifically. Local officials weren't concerned about disenfranchising Negro voters, nor were some white voters. The poll tax and literacy tests were used to help lock Blacks out of the voting process. Blacks who got into trouble with the white-run legal system also were denied voting privileges. Per the plan, these included Blacks "convicted of bribery, theft, arson, obtaining money or goods under false pretenses, perjury, forgery, embezzlement, or bigamy."

Without two dollars, impoverished Blacks were kept from voting. Blacks whose local sheriff/tax collector refused to accept their money also were denied the right to vote.

The literacy requirement meant being able to read and write any section of the constitution of the state and give a reasonable interpretation of the section to the county registrar. The applicant also was asked to show "a reasonable understanding of the duties and obligations of citizenship under a constitutional form of government."

At the discretion of the registrar, a voter applicant could be given Section 182 for "clarity." The section had enough legalese to discourage the average Black voter.

But not even violence stopped Black groups from working to increase Black voter registration under existing state constitutional rules. As more and more people nationwide reacted negatively to the blatant obstructions against Black voting in the state, the Mississippi legislature finally changed some voting requirements. Federal civil rights acts, including one in 1966, struck down more barriers.

Still, enough local Mississippi officials continued to fight against equal voting that US federal voting registrars were sent as observers in some parts of the state. The federal registrars weren't particularly welcomed in Mississippi. Local whites made little effort to cooperate with them. These federal voting registrars often searched for weeks before finding a building, storefront, or office where they could do the work they had been sent to do.

In Mendenhall, as in most other towns, the federal registrars inevitably ended up on the one piece of federal property found in most towns: the US Post Office. So the loading dock of the Mendenhall Post Office became the federal registrars' workplace in our area of the state. The dock still has marks from the studwork and plywood nailed up for a makeshift outdoor office where Blacks could register to vote.

Getting Blacks registered to vote still required extra effort, since many were concerned about their safety in doing so. Civil rights workers, including white college students who attended our meetings at Voice of Calvary, scattered out among the people.

In 1966, Voice of Calvary began voter registration and voter education activities. At the same time, we continued our regular work. We went everywhere—including small towns and farms—to talk with Blacks about registering to vote and giving them helpful information about the process. Some needed to be persuaded to do it. The fearful needed us to stand by them.

Our voter education work began in Simpson County where we lived. Smith, Jeff Davis, Copiah, and Rankin Counties were covered, too, since I had picked cotton in these places when I was younger and because Voice of Calvary currently had school projects and Bible clubs in these places.

Work in the locations continued through the summer of 1966 into 1967 and 1968. We didn't have a major influx of Blacks registering to vote, but the traffic was steady.

Whites could see a power shift taking place. The Mississippi Highway Commission—divided into northern, southern, and central highway districts—was one of the major agencies undergoing change. Mendenhall and the five counties where I had worked were in the southern district. Southern District Commissioner John D. Smith had been in office for twenty years and was an outspoken racist. I happened to live right in his hometown.

The position of highway commissioner not only offered personal prestige and political connections but also included the responsibility of hiring and firing department employees. It was an important position. In all his years of service, John Smith hadn't given in to the pressure to integrate the highway department.

In 1968, a former schoolteacher and machinery salesman named William "Shag" Pyron ran as Smith's opponent in the election. During his campaign, he invited Blacks to come talk with him. We did, and he told us that he supported Blacks being employed in the highway department. If elected, he said, Blacks would be hired. The white establishment felt uneasy about the election. The massive increase in Black registered voters could upset the system. I was among the most visible Black voters who could help upset the system in my area. The tension in Mendenhall led to anonymous angry voices over the phone:

"Perkins is a troublemaker. He's gonna get himself killed."

"Mrs. Perkins, you don't want to be a widow, do you?"

"Rev. Perkins is as good as dead right now. You better get out of town fast."

Cars we had never seen before showed up at our house at night with armed white men inside. The men would watch our house for hours at a time, edging closer and closer, waiting for any incident as an excuse for confrontation. It waged a war on our nerves, as we prayed against a confrontation that would result in gunfire.

One Sunday afternoon, I talked with community folks about the situation. After hearing what was going on, everyone agreed something had to be done. The packed church of people agreed a volunteer guard would watch our house from dusk to dawn from that day until the election.

Our guards sat or stood around the grounds of our home, wrapped in the blanket of darkness—watching, listening, and hoping that dawn would end another uneventful night. The only sounds they hoped to hear were the code words signaling that their relief had arrived, or perhaps the footsteps of one of the women bringing coffee and cookies to those on duty.

We assumed the continued visibility of guards around our house was the reason the Klan types, who had kept a silent vigil nearby, suddenly disappeared.

As for the election, Pyron defeated incumbent Smith. The new commissioner kept his promise and opened up some highway jobs for Blacks.

The election results were encouraging for Blacks in the area. Still, the agonizing processes of court litigation, voter registration, and voter education continued indefinitely.

Voice of Calvary's Leadership Development Program helped. Officially begun in 1968, this formal program integrated young leadership into each project. We had always encouraged young people to finish high school and go off to college. Now some of them were coming back for the summer.

They were especially useful in the summer tutoring program and in helping with Bible classes for younger students. In the process, they learned new skills and came to understand the importance of the work they were doing.

Having more than two million Blacks leave the Deep South between 1939 and 1964 affected the ability of Blacks to make real progress. These young, educated college students needed to know that they could make a living in Mississippi. They would help to correct the Black population issue in the South, which largely consisted of the very old and the very young. The South desperately needed these young people, who had the energy, enthusiasm, fresh ideas, and motivation to make up for the glaring age gaps of the South's Black communities. We hoped our Leadership Training Program would convince them that "you are needed here. You can have a meaningful life right here."

# The Key

**Cooperatives:** People-centered enterprises owned, controlled, and run by and for their members to realize their common economic, social, and cultural needs and aspirations. Cooperatives bring people together in a democratic and equal way.

Sometimes, my thoughts drifted back to my childhood. When they did, I saw that I spent much of it trying to escape an economic system that enslaved Black people.

Even when I was among evangelicals, I saw the same thing. I wondered if the powerless and penniless would ever actually get relief. My thinking was deeply rooted in theology, and it was about more than denouncing an old plantation system that still kept Blacks in check.

In response to this deep thinking, I added economic cooperatives (co-ops) to our voter registration activities in the mid-1960s. Several other organizers of the rural poor embraced the co-op movement as an opportunity for self-development among the poor, resulting in more than financial advances. It could provide training to help people break out of the cycle of dependence.

A conference workshop sponsored by the Southern Educational Foundation gave me further insight. I got more excited as I listened, talked, and thought about it. Apparently, these folks had high economic motivation.

As a Christian, I felt I was latching on to a promising solution to a long-standing problem. Co-ops fit neatly into my biblical understanding. But I could see that it might not have the blessing of my evangelical friends. They didn't have any framework for addressing economics from a Christian perspective.

When I thought about my brothers and sisters at the conference and the potential tension that economics could create, I wondered whether we had the spiritual strength to meet the challenge. I saw that the average strength of Christian understanding in the Black community was too weak to carry the burden. The emotional worship typical of many Black churches often lacked real Bible content.

But you can't criticize all that emotion without understanding what it did, and still does, for us as people. The strain of living in a world where you were "free" but without control over important parts of your life or matters that affected you and your community was real. The Black minister who had some skill in helping people cope with that strain and emotion helped suffering and oppressed people.

But other needs were not met, including the need for economic development.

The conference I attended helped me see the usefulness of co-ops as a tool to help bring a sense of humanity to Blacks.

So I organized the Federation of Southern Co-ops, dedicated to developing local resources and local income.

The 1960 US census classified only one-third of the housing units for Blacks in Mississippi as "sound." The remaining two-thirds were described as "dilapidated" or "deteriorating." So it was natural that housing was at the top of the list of our priorities as we began our first co-op effort in Mendenhall. A successful housing co-op would lead to improvements far beyond better housing. Ideally, it would break the cycle of despair and feelings of inferiority.

Talking to tenants living in fifteen-dollars-a-month housing was the time-consuming work that was our first order of business. Even by the most modest estimates and use of co-op efforts, I figured a decent house—a solid brick house with plumbing—would cost occupants about sixty dollars a month.

I spent months working this project into other activities, finding some families willing to organize a co-op for housing. At first, we talked about building self-help units. Using this approach, we could hire a contractor to put up a basic structure, and the owners would then put in sweat equity by finishing the interior themselves. The problem with the plan was that people willing to join the co-op had jobs. They were working—many of them long hours. This would stretch the timetable indefinitely.

Encouragement came as we learned of federal help available through the Farmers Home Administration (FmHA). "I sent letters to Washington and to local offices who had the money to fund projects to help the poor. We had the local leadership and a local organization to help carry the ball.

A couple weeks later, federal officials showed up at my house with a Black representative to work with our co-op to complete the steps necessary to get financial assistance. With the funds from local members and a loan from the FmHA, we began construction on ten duplex units. These were owned by the local co-op, which managed the funds and became the landlord of those who would pay rent. The first family moved into one of the units during the summer of 1969.

This venture was highly successful. We didn't set out to provide everyone a co-op house. We saw the co-op as the first step in better housing and home ownership in our economically depressed area.

This first step was necessary for more reasons than the obvious one of providing better housing for some. Too often, such programs simply funnel money right through the hands of the poor into the hands of the rich, without helping the poor learn how to deal with their own problems.

We saw a need for homegrown organizations to combat the cycle of discouragement, ignorance, and exploitation. Such organizations would participate in local efforts, local training, and local leadership. Many politically conservative people agree that federal government handouts don't help. People themselves must be their own economic salvation.

When we look at how the poor get poorer, two truths are evident: (1) money must be made available to develop potential, and (2) the community itself must develop its potential to multiply economic resources. In keeping with these precepts, the co-op was a school as well as a provider.

Where I lived and worked, the co-op was an economic *and* a Christian responsibility. The Bible points out how our faith should lead us to help address the physical needs of others (see Matt. 25:31–46; 1 John 3:16–18).

I want all people to come to know Jesus Christ. Nothing I do is greater than that. But I wonder why some Christians get hot under the collar when an organization like ours helps address the needs of the whole community. All people deserve economic education, even if they don't respond positively to the gospel.

With the success of the housing co-op, it was easier to organize other co-ops. Farmers in an economic pinch due to soaring prices of supplies, such as fertilizer, got relief when we developed the farmers' co-op. The co-op purchased two hundred tons of fertilizer directly from the wholesale distributor and sold it to local farmers at a big discount. The fertilizer was stored in the warehouse section of a cement-block building slated to become our next co-op operation: a co-op store.

Whatever we did was based on the needs of the people in our community. We had no way of guessing ahead of time what the reaction of the white community would be. To tell the truth, we didn't have time to care.

Besides, communication between whites and Blacks didn't happen often enough for anyone to know who was thinking what. A well-to-do white businessman considering a donation to Voice of Calvary Ministries once asked me what the local white Christians thought of our work. I told him the truth: I didn't know. In fact, I couldn't know. As a Black man, I was just as unwelcome in white churches as I was in white non-Christian organizations and homes. I told the businessman a decision would just have to be made on the merits of the project, not on the possible reaction to it.

The white churches remained silent, as far as the Black community knew. But we also had been hearing other voices, threatening voices.

I simply continued my intensive schedule: the co-ops, leadership training, Bible classes, and church activities. In the white community, the resentment grew as our accomplishments grew. We knew that sooner or later the resentment would find an excuse to explode.

As 1969 drew to a close, whites and Blacks began their usual separate preparations to celebrate the birth of the Prince of Peace.

# Disturbing the Peace

**Boycott:** When organizations or individuals voluntarily refuse to buy from or deal with a person or organization in protest. A boycott is intended to inflict some economic loss to try to change minds and objectionable actions.

**Agitating:** A campaign to arouse public concern about an issue in the hope of prompting action.

Christmas 1969 was only a couple of days away. It was just getting dark as Doug Huemmer and I turned down Main Street in Mendenhall, where holiday lights covered the white part of town. Behind us, Christmas lights twinkled on the town square and the domed county courthouse. In front of us, festive lighting lined Main Street and the rest of the landscape all the way down to the highway on the side of the railroad tracks separating the white and Black sections of town.

Stores on Main Street had all kinds of wreath and tinsel decorations for sale during the holidays. Christmas music was in the air.

*Silent night, holy night!*

We weren't driving fast. It was impossible to do so in the old, beat-up Volkswagen.

*All is calm, all is bright.*

Along the highway outside Mendenhall, signs had been posted for people passing by to read. The words of the carol sure had a different ring to them than what we saw on the road signs that night: "White people unite, defeat Jew/Communist race mixers."

*Round yon virgin, mother and Child.*

Doug and I headed to the grocery store that sold the cane syrup he wanted to take back home to his folks in California for Christmas. He planned to fly out of Jackson airport that evening. Doug had already put in a hard day's work, trying to get a lot of things finished before leaving.

*Holy infant, so tender and mild.*

Doug was a good kid, sensitive and intelligent. He was one of the young white volunteers who helped Voice of Calvary with the increased workload as we kept growing. He had stayed with us longer than many of the other volunteers.

*Sleep in heavenly peace,*
*Sleep in heavenly peace.*

Nobody in town would be surprised to see Doug and me together. Since Voice of Calvary had other white volunteers, most local whites had seen Blacks and whites together. That didn't mean they had warmed up to the idea.

Local whites were often cold toward us. Sometimes, they were even hostile when they saw me in a casual conversation with a white person as they passed by. "How are you today, Rev. Perkins?" would not be a greeting given by whites in our town anytime soon.

Doug and I pulled up to the grocery store. Inside the store, a young Black man, Garland Wilks, was trying to pay for groceries. He wasn't getting very far in convincing the white storekeeper to accept his check. He had been drinking. His voice got louder and louder.

We got Doug's syrup and paid for it. Garland was still yelling and not at all concerned about the traditional "Yessir" expected of Blacks speaking to whites. I could tell that the storekeeper and the other customers were getting annoyed. I suggested to Garland that we give him a ride home.

Thankfully, he agreed. Doug and I escorted him outside into our car. We got in quickly and slammed the doors. Garland's rowdy behavior in the store could have easily become an ugly confrontation.

I didn't know that the angry grocer had already phoned the police. We were heading for Garland's house with Doug driving when a patrol car came up behind us. I got a little tense—a natural reaction for a Black person in the South.

The police followed us to the dirt road leading to the Black section of town. We weren't far from the Voice of Calvary building when the patrol car's flashing blue lights signaled us to pull over. We did.

Doug hopped out of the car faster than I did, asking the officer, "Is something wrong?"

Another officer yelled, "You shut up! Stand aside!"

Leaning inside the open door of our VW, another officer said, "Come out of there, Garland. You're under arrest!"

"Under arrest for what?" I asked.

"Public drunkenness and disturbing the peace."

Disturbing the peace! That handy catch-all charge was commonly used.

"But he's in the car with us. He's not disturbing the peace."

The officer snapped, "You shut up!"

Doug and I promised to take Garland home ourselves.

"Just shut up!"

There was nothing more we could do. Garland got out of the VW and climbed into the patrol car. I told Doug, "You drive straight to Voice of Calvary. I'm going to go tell Garland's grandma what has happened. I'll walk home from there."

I promised Garland's grandma that I would see about his bail. Back at VOC, our college students, home for the holidays, and local students were busy rehearsing for a Christmas pageant. I told Carolyn Albritton what had happened. She told me that Roy Berry had been arrested earlier that day as he came out of church and was beaten badly. But it wasn't until much later that anybody knew what Roy had done to break the law.

"He ain't done nothin', Rev. Perkins," Carolyn said. "They claimed he was making phone calls to a white woman, asking her for a date. They took him down to jail and beat him. They said they ought to kill him!"

Somebody had decided that Roy Berry was the guilty party. Nobody knew how or why. For now, the only obvious fact was that a young Black man had been grabbed and beaten by "the law." With Garland Wilks also being arrested, only the Lord knew what would happen next.

Carolyn burst into tears. "They gonna beat up Garland, too!"

I believed Carolyn. I'd lived through enough outbreaks of police brutality in Mendenhall to know the truth when I heard it. Ever since Blacks started agitating in the early '60s, white hatred had been rising. Emotions had swelled to a breaking point, and the results could be catastrophic.

With the Christmas rehearsal finished, I suggested we go see how things turned out for Garland. Doug and I took the whole group uptown to the police station in City Hall. It seemed to be the wisest move to make at the time. Seventeen of us, including junior high kids, surely would not be jailed. Four of my own children were in that nervous, noisy group.

We got to City Hall in three cars. Stores were still open late for last-minute Christmas shoppers. We pulled into the City Hall parking lot. Mendenhall's police chief, Mark Sherman, met us in the parking lot. One teenager asked right away, "Did you beat up Garland?"

"We ain't laid a hand on him," the chief assured us. "He's over there in the car." We looked, and Garland was still sitting in the back of the patrol car.

"But you beat up my cousin, Roy Berry, this afternoon," the girl insisted.

"Mendenhall police had nothing to do with that case," the chief responded. "The county sheriff took that one. You'll have to go on over to the jail to see for yourself."

Some of our crowd walked and others rode to the Mendenhall jail. The jailer and his family lived in the same building, with their front door opening off of the jail's front entrance hall. All seventeen of us walked into the jail building together, surprising and upsetting the jailer, Mr. Griffiths, and his wife.

"We came to see Roy Berry," we told him.

More people joined the seventeen of us, but they waited outside by their cars. In the lobby of the jail, a debate was brewing as we continued our confrontation with the jailer.

Griffiths walked into the booking office just off the lobby. About twelve of us followed him. We could see that he was getting scared, but we didn't expect him to say, "You're all under arrest." He opened the big steel doors to the cell block.

If this was the only way we would see Roy, then so be it. Doug stepped forward. The jailer grabbed him and shoved him through the door. I walked in behind him and the others followed. Unbelievably, all of us had been arrested!

The jailer didn't quite know what the next step would be. He was pretty sure he'd at least removed the personal threat that he felt. After we were securely behind bars, the jailer called the county sheriff and the highway patrol. They asked him if he knew who the demonstrators were. His reply was, "A minister, a white social worker, and some kids." The jailer arrested all of us without using proper procedures and without stating any clear charges.

Without admitting he was wrong, the jailer looked at us through the cell bars and asked the kids if they were ready to go. He would let most of them go free, he said.

The kids wanted to know why they'd been locked up in the first place. The jailer didn't say. The kids and the jailer argued back and forth for a while until the jailer went back to his desk without providing any clarity. The patrolmen, the county sheriff, and the district attorney arrived soon after the jailer called the sheriff. The state highway patrol had almost doubled in size in 1964, when Mississippi claimed to fear mass disturbances in view of civil rights activities. The highway patrol used its power as a last-stand attempt to preserve their Southern traditions of white superiority. Any call for help in a racial situation would bring a quick response by patrol cars. That's exactly what happened when the Mendenhall jailer called for help.

Our group of supporters who had stayed outside the jail went back to the church to tell everyone there what had happened. A crowd of our people and folks from all over the county responded by gathering outside the jail.

White officials hadn't planned on things turning out quite the way they did, but the situation had happened and they would never admit any mistakes. Their best bet was to back up the actions of the jailer. So the highway patrolmen talked with the jailer for a while. A large officer approached the bars of the jail cell. "Tell you what, kids," he said. "If you leave nice and easy, nobody will be hurt. We just want to keep Rev. Perkins and this Huemmer fella overnight. But you kids can get out of here." No one moved. One teenager announced, "We ain't goin' no place without Rev. Perkins and Doug. They didn't do anything that we didn't do. So either let us all out, or we all will stay." The others nodded their heads in agreement.

The patrolman cursed and went back to the group of officers. They discussed what to do next. Meanwhile, more people were gathering around the front of the jail. Inside the jail, we could hear our people outside demanding explanations. Vera Mae was in the crowd, wondering what was happening to the children and me.

There wasn't a lot Vera Mae or the others could do except to stay outside in the dark, praying and crying and wondering what was happening inside. With the jail being upstairs, they couldn't see inside. But they could hear the children crying.

The authorities struggled to figure out what to do next. With kids in jail, the crowd outside grew much larger than before. But the size of the crowd wasn't the biggest concern for the white officials. The main Black leadership of Simpson County was in that crowd outside the jail, and that was a problem for them. I also knew that major Black leadership in the county was there, having seen them from the window. Beating us up would not go over well for the white officers.

They would use that kind of tactic only when no one else was around.

Vera Mae wasn't sure what to do. She just knew she had to be there. She overheard a white patrolman tell the Blacks in the crowd that I was a false preacher, that I was misleading people, and that they ought to turn against me. His words that evening only helped solidify our distrust of whites.

From the jail window, I could hear the crowd of Blacks below arguing my case among themselves. I knew this could go on all night. I felt utterly helpless. I pondered on what I could say that would make a difference.

I felt anxiety, anguish, pity, and grief. Somehow, love was a part of that equation, too. It was so deep and so strong that I couldn't contain it.

Through the bars of the window, I spoke to the crowd in the street below. I wanted to let them know that I cared very much about all of them. I knew they cared about me. They also were angry about my current circumstances, enough to do something about it.

I begged the leaders in the crowd not to do anything we would all regret, reminding them that if we gave in now to anger, violence, and hate, we would be just like the white folks—doing the very same things to them that they were doing to us. They would be the winners and we would be the losers if we returned hate for hate, anger for anger, and violence for violence. Taking that route also would cause us to lose what little we had gained and would wipe out any hope for further progress.

The power and emotions of my words that night were so strong that I don't remember everything I said. I do remember that my heart was in every word spoken. Even as our people were warned that we risked hurting ourselves by seeking revenge, I also added that we could hurt ourselves *and* our children's future if we did nothing. Clearly, the legal system was working against us. We had to take a stand for ourselves. Someplace. Sometime.

The place was here, and the time was now.

I didn't want to do anything to add to their suffering. They had already experienced too much suffering in their lives. I told them that *I* was willing to do the suffering at this point, and even ready to die, if necessary.

But the truth is, whether I lived, suffered behind bars, or died would not have as great an impact as uniting the Black community in seeking progress *together*. Taking a united stand would stimulate real change. Timing was critical, and that very moment was the time to unite members of the Black community for real progress.

As I spoke, I prayed that other Blacks would come to understand and feel as I did about our communities, that they would understand what I was saying and why. The major issues that the Black community wanted to bring to the attention of local officials were not being addressed. No Blacks worked anywhere in uptown Mendenhall except as janitors, domestics, and cooks. We wanted better jobs for Black people. Better living conditions. Paved streets. Simply put, we wanted a better life for our people, for all people.

As I was speaking, the idea of a boycott came to mind. An economic boycott! Why not? In a small town like Mendenhall, where political and business interests were essentially the same, the idea of Blacks staying away from the stores made a lot of sense. With the Christmas shopping rush, a boycott of stores could make quite a difference.

The Black community had placed a lot of items on layaway until Christmas Eve. I asked that everyone in town with items on layaway leave them there and that they stop shopping in Mendenhall until the town started hurting financially. Perhaps when the whites began to suffer financially, they would listen to us and begin to understand how much we were hurting, too.

I said all of that. Then I stopped and waited.

The youngsters still presented the most sensitive problem for the police. They had provided a background of controlled chaos throughout my "speech." When it was over, the officers decided to remove the kids from jail by force, leaving only Doug and me. We were still under arrest, they said.

The kids didn't go quietly. They were yelling, "No, no. I won't go!" The police resorted to grabbing them by their arms and legs, lifting them off the floor, and taking them all outside. One by one, officers carried the teenagers and the younger kids out of the jail. Doug and I remained locked securely in the jail cell. The patrolmen sealed off the door and refused to let anyone else inside.

Nothing more could be settled that night. Doug and I were charged and locked up around two o'clock in the morning. The exact charges would be disputed later at the trial.

The district attorney left, and the crowd outside the jailhouse eventually broke up and headed home. Doug and I were officially in jail.

The cell was bare. The floor was hard.

*All is calm, all is bright.*

I had trouble sleeping that night.

# Green Power

**Warrant:** A document issued by a legal or government official authorizing the police or some other body to make an arrest, search premises, or carry out some other action relating to the administration of justice.

**Bond/Bail:** The words *bail* and *bond* are often used almost interchangeably when discussing jail release. They are closely related but not the same thing. Bail is the money a defendant must pay in order to get out of jail. A bond is posted on a defendant's behalf, usually by a bail bond company, to secure his or her release.

fter the crowd left the jailhouse, Vera Mae, the college students, and the younger kids went back to the church. The idea of a boycott gave them just what they needed to stand up to the white man. They were angry and anxious to get it going, but they knew that a boycott without organization and strategy would not work.

Later, Vera Mae filled me in on what happened that night. Even as the young folks talked, all noisy and nervous-like, they were already making picket signs out of anything they could get their hands on. They stayed up all night sawing wooden slats, cutting up cardboard boxes, pasting down the cardboard, and using up one Magic Marker after another to write the signs they would carry during the boycott.

At sunup, the boycott was ready to roll. By eight o'clock that morning, Vera Mae and kids from VOC were uptown, peacefully picketing the stores and announcing a total boycott of all businesses. They made it clear that the boycott would go on as long as necessary.

Vera Mae wasn't too sure at first what she should do. The idea of a boycott was new to her. But she stood on the corner across from the bank, right where cars with shoppers coming into town slowed down to stop or make a turn. If Black people were in a car, she would go to them and say, "We ain't shoppin' in Mendenhall this Christmas."

They'd ask, "Why, honey? What happened?"

She'd reply, "They got Brother Perkins and Doug in jail for no reason and ain't doin' nothin' about it. Go shop in Jackson or somewhere else."

Having to shop in other towns was hard for some people because they already had money deposited on layaway items in Mendenhall. But people were willing to forfeit their money laid away for bicycles, sewing machines, and other merchandise. As much as Vera Mae could see, the Mendenhall boycott had the total cooperation of Blacks from all over the county and even outside the county, too.

None of our people passed Vera Mae and went into any store. That made her feel good. It meant the Black community was pulling together. The Black community was taking a stand. The boycott was making an impact.

In fact, the boycott worked so well that it surprised everybody. No Black shoppers and only a few whites could be found on the streets. You could see orderly groups of picketers at key locations in the business district. Blacks in town weren't the only ones honoring the boycott by staying away from the stores. When whites saw the picketers up and down Main Street, most of them stayed away, too.

Whites, who didn't want Blacks in politics, still needed our business dollars. No last-minute Christmas shopping. No layaway pickup. On the day before Christmas, this boycott was bad news for store owners.

By ten o'clock that morning, frustrated storekeepers pressured the police and town officials to do something, anything, to get rid of the Perkins case. The sheriff came to me and pleaded with me to make bond to get out of jail.

I knew it was a trick. The initiative for making bond is up to the jailed person, and I had made no such request.

The police and officials were under pressure. Mendenhall businesses were losing money. As a prisoner, I had become a real liability to town officials.

"I can't make bond," I told them. "I can't do anything without a lawyer."

"Then call him and get him down here to the jail."

I called my lawyer in Jackson. "You stay there," he told me. "Make 'em sweat. Christmas Eve—just before nightfall—make bail then."

The officials kept trying to hurry me out of the jail. Of course, the quickest way—dropping the charges—was out of the question from their standpoint. Instead, they sent some Blacks to urge me to come out—Blacks they thought might be willing to forget injustice in the name of cooperation. But I convinced each one of them of the importance of what we were doing.

On Christmas Eve, after the stores were closed, Doug and I announced we would make bail and come out of the jail cell. Everybody tried to pretend that this Christmas was like other Christmases. But we knew a new road had been taken. Whites could no longer control the Black community the same way they had always done, and especially as long as the charges against me were unsettled.

The facts of our arrest remained unsettled, along with the charges. So the boycott—our selective buying campaign—continued and grew, with more and more Blacks from Mendenhall and other nearby towns participating.

A carefully thought-out list of demands was presented by the Black community. It started with dropping all charges against Perkins, Huemmer, and Roy Berry (the young man arrested and beaten).

Next, it covered American civil rights, which Black Americans had always struggled for.

*We demand* that police obey the US Constitution and Supreme Court orders.

*We demand* that persons be given due process rights under the law when arrested: advised of their rights, given the right to remain silent, the right to immediate bail, the right to a phone call, the right to an attorney, and the right to clean and healthy confinement.

*We demand* that the police, sheriffs, and highway patrol must have a sworn warrant before arresting a person or searching a house or car.

*We demand* that streets in the Black community be paved.

Mishandling by law enforcement officers was an ever-present fear. But many problems were in the area of employment and the simple opportunity to earn a living. No Blacks were in municipal government, the welfare office, the jails, the school board, the draft board, the city police, government offices, or serving as court reporters. Addressing these areas was on our list of demands. Adherence to the minimum wage was also on the list, especially for those who worked as maids. We also sought desegregation of all public facilities, including the schools. (Schools were desegregated under court order the following year.)

The whites refused to discuss our list of demands.

Overall, the arrests and the refusal to admit any mistakes in the handling of the whole affair opened a floodgate of emotions in the Black community. But through it all, there was nothing illegal or violent in either the list of demands or the method of dramatizing them. All activities in the Black community were conducted according to plan. There would be no random acts of violence or call for anything that would step outside the law. We only demanded rights that were supposed to be guaranteed to all American citizens under the Constitution.

The boycott continued through January and February. Every Saturday during those months, leaders of the Black community used a parade permit to hold a march. The march began at Voice of Calvary in the Black section of town, continued across the railroad tracks onto Main Street, circled around the courthouse, and returned.

*"Do right, white man, do right. Do right, white man, do right."*

To that rhythmic chant, a group of us (Nathan Rubin, Curry Brown, Jesse Newsome, Vera Mae, and I) led the marches, walking in front of the lines. Yes, we were afraid. We faced highway patrolmen and sheriffs armed with shotguns, gas masks, and billy clubs. At the same time, God gave us courage that we didn't normally have. We did what we had to do, and we knew God was with us.

The worst thing about the hypocrisy in the South was that whites, who called themselves Christians, were also staunch racists who actively or passively participated in discrimination and enslavement through unfair and unlawful practices. The troubling question on my mind and on the minds of most Black people we preached to was whether Christianity was a stronger force than racism.

The weekly parade drew more and more participants. College students from Jackson State and nearby Tougaloo College joined in, adding momentum to the VOC campaign against oppression. On some Saturdays, as many as two hundred chanting young Blacks made their way up and down Main Street.

*"Do right, white man, do right. Do right, white man, do right."*

The mood of Blacks on the days of the marches was one of triumph and excitement. But whites remained angry, resentful, and resistant.

Some Blacks lost their jobs. Companies canceled the fire insurance policies on the homes of others. Nevertheless, the boycott went on. The white community remained unwilling to negotiate with Black leaders or to admit the botched-up handling of "the Perkins arrest."

In the meantime, boycott leaders organized carpools to take Blacks on shopping trips to Jackson. Some of them never went back to buying in local stores, even after the boycott ended.

The response pushed forward the opening date of a co-op that had been in the works for some time, the Simpson County Co-op Store. It was owned and operated by local Blacks.

While no action was taken against any Black leader or members of the Black community during the boycott, we all were under constant surveillance by the sheriff and the state highway patrol. Cameramen photographed people participating in the marches. Observers kept records of every move we made.

Photos for what? Records for what?

We would soon find out.

# Ambush

## 17

**Demonstration:** A nonviolent direct-action protest such as marches, rallies, picketing, sit-ins, and boycotts.

**Freedom songs:** Political songs sung by enslaved or oppressed people who oppose a cruel or unfair government or society.

On Saturday, February 7, 1970, Doug Huemmer and I drove to Tougaloo College near Jackson to pick up a group of students attending college there. These Tougaloo students supported the Mendenhall boycott and planned to join in our march later that day.

Highway 49 was the main road in and out of Mendenhall. In town, Highway 13 was the main road in and out of the section of Mendenhall where Blacks lived. The police had set up roadblocks and driver's license checkpoints on Highway 49,

Highway 13, and all other roads leading in and out of Mendenhall.

This made the trip from Voice of Calvary back and forth to Tougaloo somewhat risky and dangerous since we had to pass through these control points manned by the police. We were being closely monitored every Saturday, and we knew it.

In Mendenhall, we rallied with other demonstrators at our new co-op store and planned last-minute details for the march. When everybody was ready, we took up our signs, formed our parade, and headed for the center of town—100 to 150 strong.

The march took us past the roadblock and through the checkpoint. Long lines of our demonstrators walked up and down Main Street, chanting our theme message: *"Do right, white man, do right. Do right, white man, do right."*

We demonstrated in town for about forty-five minutes. While we marched, white bystanders heckled us. State officials who were looking on took pictures. Sheriff's deputies and highway patrolmen with gas masks and weapons were standing along the march route, watching our every move.

After the march through town, we came back to VOC and held a meeting at our church. Afterward, nineteen Tougaloo students got into a Dodge van driven by Doug Huemmer for the ride back to Jackson. The rest of the college students piled into VOC's Volkswagen van driven by Louise Fox. The two vans, with Doug leading and Louise following, left Mendenhall on Highway 49, traveling northwest out of town. A Mississippi Highway Patrol car followed the vans.

The college students were in high spirits. They clapped their hands and sang freedom songs. They also joked about the state officials with their zoom lens cameras snapping pictures of the marchers. They even laughed about the police standing guard with nightsticks and shotguns along the route. The upbeat mood led a student to start saying the chant again, and others chimed in: *"Do right, white man, do right. Do right, white man, do right."*

At about six thirty, as the sun was just going down, the two vans rolled across the Rankin County line. Immediately, near the town of Plain, a highway patrol car cut in between the VW van in the rear and Doug's van in front. The patrol car's blue lights signaled Doug to pull over and stop.

Right away, Doug smelled trouble. For a routine violation, the driver was usually ticketed and sent on. But Doug sensed this was not routine. They were away from the community now. There just might be complications.

Doug waved to Louise and the folks in the other van to keep on going. He figured they might need to call me. But Louise pulled off the highway and stopped to see what would happen.

Doug pulled the Dodge van onto the shoulder of the road and parked. The patrol car parked behind Doug. A patrolman named Douglas O. Baldwin got out and walked up to the van, ordering Doug to get out, produce his driver's license, and get into the patrol car.

Doug obeyed. What happened next and the details of what was said would later be on official record.

Baldwin said, "You almost hit a pickup." This was not true. Then Baldwin saw the Tougaloo students looking out of the rear windows of the van.

"Are you some of the demonstrators from Mendenhall?" He smiled slightly. "Well, we're not going to take any more of this civil rights stuff." The patrolman called on his radio, saying that he had Doug and the others and that they were armed. "Come help me take 'em in."

Doug asked him if he was under arrest. Baldwin told him that if he didn't shut up, he was going to shoot him in the head.

Doug shut up.

A few minutes later, several Mississippi Highway Patrol cars arrived at the scene in response to the radio request. With pistols drawn, the patrolmen ordered the students out of the van.

With all those blue lights flashing in the night mist and radios crackling and buzzing, it was an eerie sight. The patrolmen lined the nineteen students up against the van, spread their legs, and frisked them. While they roughly searched the kids, they cussed at them. The patrolmen called them agitators, among other humiliating and derogatory names.

One student spoke up and told the patrolmen that not one of their college friends would be arrested unless all of them were. He got his wish. Patrolman Baldwin placed them all under arrest, handcuffing and transporting them to the Rankin County Jail in Brandon—a few miles east of Jackson.

Doug was handcuffed and taken in a separate car and beaten, both on the way to and after arriving at the jail. Once parked outside the jail, the patrolmen hit Doug in his face and neck and twisted him around in the car to punch him in his stomach and groin. Baldwin kept saying he'd warned Doug. "I wanted to kill you tonight; that's what I wanted to do." But he said he was going to teach Doug a lesson instead. They continued slapping and kicking him.

Inside the Brandon jail, all of the Tougaloo College students were booked on charges ranging from "reckless driving" to "carrying a concealed deadly brick." The officers taunted them, kicked them, and beat them with blackjacks.

Meanwhile, as soon as the highway patrolmen drove away with Doug and the students, Louise Fox got to a phone in Plain and called us in Mendenhall. We could hear fear in her trembling voice. She was crying. "The people in Doug's van have been locked up in Brandon."

I told Louise to take the rest of the students on to Tougaloo College. Rev. Curry Brown, Joe Paul Buckley, and I set out for Brandon and the Rankin County Jail, planning to post bail for Doug and the students. All of them had clearly been victims of an ambush on Highway 49. Yet the same police officers who arrested them just let Louise and her load of passengers go free. Why? Could it be because they knew she would call us and tell us to come? Was there another ambush out there on that highway—waiting for us?

We had to go, regardless.

When Curry, Joe Paul, and I got to the courthouse and jail, a highway patrolman outside showed us where to park. We got out of the car and stood beside it.

"We'd like to see the sheriff," we told the patrolman.

"Okay," he said. "I'll go tell him you're here."

Instead of the sheriff coming to see us, about a dozen highway patrolmen came out of the building, searched us, and arrested us.

It was an ambush after all, only it was here at the jail, not on Highway 49. We'd fallen right into their trap.

Even before they got us into the building, the police started beating us. Curry caught it bad right away from Officer Frank Thames while he was being taken into the jail. Thames kicked him in the back and the kidney all the way. Then it got worse.

At least five deputy sheriffs and seven to twelve highway patrolmen went to work on the three of us. Sheriff Edwards also joined in. One Tougaloo student said he saw Sheriff Edwards beat me so hard his shirttail came out. During the beatings, I tried to cover my head with my arms, but they beat me till I was lying on the floor in a pool of blood. Even then, they kept on beating and stomping me, kicking me in the head, in the ribs, in the groin. I rolled up in a ball to protect myself as best I could.

The beatings just went on and on. Would the agony never end?

Several deputies took a break from the beatings and sipped moonshine whiskey from paper cups before getting back to work on us for what seemed like hours during the night. At one point, the sheriff's deputies shaved the heads of both Curry and Doug. Then Sheriff Edwards poured moonshine whiskey all over Doug's head.

Because I was unconscious most of the time, I don't remember much about the others. I don't even remember a whole lot about what happened to me, except that there was blood all over the place, and a lot of it was mine. I know that some of the students were beaten, too.

Doug was also unconscious a good deal of the time, suffering from blows to his head. But he saw and remembered enough to testify later. He remembered the drunken officers beating on several of us with a leather blackjack. He testified that they dragged me all across the floor, kicking and beating me the worst.

Word came over the radio that the FBI might be coming. Well, it wouldn't do to have blood all over the floor while entertaining the FBI. So they ordered me to take a mop and start cleaning up.

I did my best, but I was so weak and wobbly. I was in so much pain. Blood was still pouring from my head, and it didn't help that some of the police kept on beating me as I tried to mop up my own blood. Then they had me go into a back room to wash up nice and clean for our federal visitors.

No FBI came. The false report angered the patrolmen even more than before. They cursed me and began beating me again, making up for lost time. The threat of the FBI coming in had reminded them of at least some legal niceties. They took me to another room, photographed me, and started taking my fingerprints.

Even then, they wouldn't stop the torture. While they were taking my prints, one officer took a pistol, put it to my head, and pulled the trigger. Then another officer beat me unconscious again.

After I came to, the officers decided they wanted a performance. They had found a copy of the printed demands of the Black community of Mendenhall. They ordered me to read the demands aloud as entertainment for the party.

I was in no shape to do it. My eyes were swollen shut. I could barely see anything through the blood that streamed down my face. I was having real trouble even breathing. My throat was all banged up and swollen. I couldn't read loud enough to suit them.

"Read louder, nigga!" they shouted as they cursed and humiliated me.

I don't know how long all this went on or which officer did what. I do remember that it got worse as the night wore on. I couldn't have imagined this kind of situation happening. One officer took a bent fork and shoved it up my nose, then pushed it down my throat. Then they beat me down to the floor again.

It was a night of horror. I can't forget their faces, so twisted with hate. It was like looking at demons. Hate did that to them.

At that moment, looking into a chasm of hate, I couldn't hate back. When I saw what hate had done to them, I couldn't do the same. I could only pity them. I didn't ever want hate to do to me what it did to those men.

At long last, the awful beatings and torture stopped. I was taken upstairs and put into the hands of two jailers who hadn't been in on the other beatings. I guess they wanted to get their licks in, too, because they started beating me on the way to the cell. By this time, my head and body were numb. I only vaguely remember that some of the Tougaloo students helped me onto a cot. Things seemed strangely out of balance.

Throughout the rest of that night, I drifted in and out of consciousness as pain flooded back and forth through my body. A student's shirt, soaked in cold water, was carefully placed on my swollen head. The students cared for me the rest of the night.

Someone called Vera Mae and told her the three of us had been locked up. She knew nothing about the physical and mental torture we endured that night in Brandon. She was home in bed, feeling afraid, sleepless, and altogether helpless.

Around one o'clock in the morning, the phone rang. A man's voice wickedly asked, "Have they hung him yet?"

"Hung who?" Vera Mae cried.

The caller hung up.

Vera Mae got to Brandon about nine o'clock the next morning. When she and others arrived, a crowd of white men were standing and sitting around the jailhouse. They were folks we'd call Klan types. They casually stood around, on the alert, seeing everything and missing nothing. Some were chewing and spitting tobacco. A half smile was on their faces.

Vera Mae, Mrs. Buckley, Larry Buckley, Mrs. Stanfield, and others came to the jailhouse. Joe Paul, looking out of one of the upper windows in the jail section, saw them coming.

"Go back!" he yelled. "Don't let Larry and those other boys in here. The sheriff said he'd shoot them!"

I knew they'd be scared. Anybody with sense would be scared. But they went on into the jailhouse.

Sheriff Edwards met them. "Ain't nobody going in but the mothers and wives. So, all you other folks, go on back outside."

Mrs. Buckley said, "I'm Joe Paul's wife."

"My son's in there," said Mrs. Stanfield.

"I'm Mrs. Perkins," Vera Mae told the sheriff.

The officers led me to the room where Vera Mae was waiting. I was so weak and in so much pain, I couldn't stand. They had to give me a chair before I collapsed to the floor. Vera Mae stood with a policeman only inches behind her. We could have no privacy. Whatever Vera Mae was feeling and thinking, she was determined to hide it. I looked horrible. Vera Mae could see the swollen wounds, bruises, blood, and bulging eyes. In the background, the younger students yelled. There was no way she couldn't hear them.

Vera Mae positioned her arms and shoulders as big as she could, reaching down and around me so The Man couldn't hear.

"What happened to you?" she whispered quietly.

"Vera Mae," I said, "get me out of here because they gonna kill me." I couldn't say much more than that.

"Toop, honey, let me see what I can do."

Only later did Vera Mae learn from some of the Tougaloo students, who had nursed me through the night, that they were sure I was dead—or about to die.

But right then, with all of us still behind bars, it was time to work. Mr. Nathan Rubin, Civic League president of Simpson County, started looking for Blacks with property willing to post bonds. Men like J. D. Hill, John Adams, Henry Griffin, and M. J. Mangum willingly put up their property. Other friends offered to help, too, but none of them owned enough property to cover the bonds.

All of them were turned away.

Finally, an old lady and friend, Alfoncia Hill, offered to put up her farm and many acres to cover my bond. She walked bravely into Sheriff Edwards's office, signed the bond, and walked out. I was released about three o'clock that Sunday afternoon.

I'll never forget the gigantic dimensions of these noble tributes. But there still wasn't enough bond for everyone. We needed a $5,000 bond alone just for Curry. Even with his terrible head injuries, Curry had to spend all Sunday night in jail. The officers continued to taunt him throughout the night. They told him that all his friends had deserted him and that no one was coming back to get him.

Around five o'clock on Monday, we got Curry Brown out of jail. He was the last one out.

Mr. Luvell Purvis, who lived not too far from the Brandon jail, not only helped raise our bail but also opened up his house to the released prisoners as we gradually bailed everybody out. His home became a sanctuary, like the home of John Mark's mother in the book of Acts where they joyfully welcomed Peter after he was released from prison.

Mr. Purvis was a barber. Carefully, gently, he trimmed the hair away from my wounds. In every way, this quiet, dignified man did all he could to ease the anguish each of us had suffered.

I was still in the house when Curry was brought in. He had probably suffered more than any of us. For a long moment, we could only look at each other. After that, we wrapped our arms around each other and hugged and cried.

*Dear God, the nightmare was over.*

We were free.

# Beyond Brandon

**Systemic:** Something that is spread throughout, affecting a group or system, such as a body, economy, market, or society as a whole.

Long after the Brandon jail incident, our hearts and bodies were still bruised. Healing would come slowly. We were all badly wounded physically and emotionally. Many of us had lost a lot of blood. One student's teeth had been knocked out. Curry had deep cuts in the back of his head. I had injuries all over my body. A week later, the knot of blood on my head was so big and soft, the doctor had to draw out almost a cup of fluid to get it to go down.

Our injuries were treated by Dr. Robert Smith, a good friend and dedicated Black physician. We kept him busy for a while. As a Black professional, Dr. Smith could have set up shop in lots of other places where the work was easier and the pay higher. But he stayed and set up practice here in Mississippi. He participated in marches in Jackson and around the state. He believed in our cause and was fully involved in the movement.

I remember one conversation Dr. Smith shared with me. After attending a medical conference at a local hotel, a white colleague was trying to tell him how well things had progressed in Black-white relations. The white doctor pointed out that they were now able to attend the same medical conventions, eat at the same restaurants, and, in general, have more contact than in previous years.

"Who knows," the white doctor added, "maybe not too long from now you will even be able to attend our church."

The doctor's statement was straightforward. Obviously, it never entered that white churchman's mind that progress in Black-white relations should begin—not end—in the church. Nor did he seem aware that many of the most systematic haters were ministers and Sunday school teachers.

One Sunday, Curry and Doug went to a white church in Mendenhall. They joined with the rest of the congregation in the singing of the "Doxology."

*Praise God, from whom all blessings flow.*

Clomp, clomp, clomp! Over the sound of the music came the loud thuds of feet stomping up the aisle. It was the chief of police.

*Praise Him, all creatures here below.*

The chief stopped at Curry and Doug's pew. "You weren't invited here. The congregation, the minister, and I don't want you here. Get out!"

*Praise Him above, ye heavenly host.*

They got out!

*Praise Father, Son, and Holy Ghost.*

At Brandon, the white community had made it clear that it would go to any length—even to the brink of murder—to prevent Blacks from having their rights. I saw then that the result of Black agitation was a hardening of white attitudes, not the softening of hearts as I had hoped.

Other incidences told us exactly where we stood.

A few days after Brandon, Curry sent someone to pick up his van at the garage where the police had towed it. The attendant said he had orders from the sheriff to let no one but the owner pick it up. Also, he was supposed to call the sheriff so the sheriff could come before the vehicle was released.

That seemed odd to Curry. So later on, he went down to the garage himself. A white civil rights worker went with him. The attendant called the sheriff's office and learned the sheriff was tied up in court. Contrary to the sheriff's specific orders, he let the vehicle go.

The next day Curry went to his van to get some tools. A few minutes later he came into the house where Vera Mae was working, his hand shaking like a leaf. And in his hand, he held a deadly sharp straight razor.

He had found the razor in one of his work boots. But it wasn't his. He had never seen it before. Someone had placed it there.

"Sister Perkins," he said to Vera Mae, "now I understand why they didn't let Herbert pick up my van the other day. They were going to follow me and arrest me somewhere along the road. Then they'd search my van and find this 'concealed weapon.' Sister Perkins, they were going to kill me!"

In the following weeks, whenever the local patrolmen slowly cruised by VOC and saw Curry working outside, they would wave their shotguns at him as a reminder of who was boss in this town.

Just a reminder.

After Brandon, I started wondering more about white folks. After all, they're humans just like us. All of us are made in the image of God, even though the image has gotten pretty bent and cracked at times.

People don't do anything without some sort of reason. Take that whole Brandon mess. It was something you wouldn't dream people could do to each other. But they did. Why?

Before Brandon, the reasons weren't very clear. But after I was beaten by white policemen, I began to see things a little more clearly. I was able to see the brokenness of white people and the damage that racism was doing to them. I had gotten used to the fact that the sickness of racism had kept the Black community from functioning as a healthy community. A lot of our people were sick—affected by generations of slavery, oppression, and exploitation—psychologically destroyed. But I had never thought much about how all that had affected whites: how they too had been affected by racism, by attitudes of racial superiority, by unjust lifestyles and behavior.

Now I wondered a lot.

There was nothing unique about the Brandon beatings. There have been plenty like them—beatings by police officers and patrolmen, not just by mobs.

I don't think most white Americans of that day would believe that what happened to us in Brandon still happened at that time in America. I wouldn't expect them to believe that the police and the highway patrol had deliberately planned that ambush and how they had treated us. Whites would probably have said, "It's almost too much to believe. Who would be so stupid as to beat someone like that in jail?"

And most white Christians would not have wanted to believe such a situation could happen either. They would have closed their eyes to it. Why? Because if a white person minded his own business, he went up the ladder in society. So he figured that a Black guy who got in trouble must have been guilty of disobeying the law. (Decades later, too many still think this way.)

But "it ain't necessarily so."

And what of the law officers themselves? I wondered about them, too.

Some white people have nothing going for themselves in life except their whiteness, their sense of superiority and racism. Too often, this kind of person is attracted to law enforcement. There, he gets a chance to make himself feel important by brutalizing a Black person.

Everyone has a need for significance. Sadly, brutality is sometimes like a drug. Some people have to have it to reassure themselves of their importance. Not all policemen are like this. But *sometimes* the occupation attracts this kind of person to the uniform, and I don't see any effective effort to keep such types out.

Say you're Black and you're stopped by a white highway patrolman. If the officer happens to be one of the types I'm referring to, he'll ask you questions. But he doesn't really want to talk with you, so his questions are just ones to which you respond, "yes, sir" or "no, sir." And after you've answered all his questions, he may make you repeat the answers. It satisfies his need for authority.

The point is, Blacks don't have to be militant to have trouble with the law. Any action by them—or no action at all—can be seen as "hostility." When that happens, there is no such thing as Blacks having a choice of violence or nonviolence. Hostility

and violence are interpreted for them. Blackness is unfortunately a hostile threat to whiteness. That kind of problem is
what white conservative Christians, miles from the situation,
miss entirely when they criticize efforts or projects by Blacks
aimed at common human dignity.

Do you see why I wonder?

# Mississippi Justice

**Appeal:** In legal terms, an appeal is a challenge to a previous legal determination or judgment.

**Contributing to the delinquency of a minor:** A crime that can be charged when a person acts or fails to act in a way that causes a minor (a person under the age of eighteen) to engage in illegal or delinquent behavior.

**Statute:** A written law passed by a legislative body.

**Reversible error:** A legal mistake at the trial court level that is so significant (resulted in an improper judgment) that the judgment must be reversed by the appellate (or higher) court.

ine days after the Brandon incident, I started down the long legal road of *Perkins v. The State of Mississippi*. I would face a nonjury trial before a justice of the peace, without knowing what the charge was against me. Neither did my lawyers.

All we knew was that the charge stemmed from the night of December 23, 1969, when Doug and I were arrested and detained overnight in the Mendenhall jail. No one told me of any statute I had violated. This made it tough for my lawyers to prepare a case for my defense.

My lawyers knew we would lose our case in Mendenhall, no matter what the evidence might be. Their strategy was to make enough objections to buy me a chance for appeal to a higher court.

On February 16, 1970, I went before the justice of the peace. His verdict was based only on his finding that I had performed certain alleged actions. How these actions broke a law was never discussed. The quick verdict: guilty, with punishment of a $300 fine and three months in the county jail.

We appealed. A person who appeals a justice of the peace verdict and asks for a trial by jury gets a new trial altogether. So a month later—on March 16, 1970—my new trial began with Circuit Court Judge Joseph A. McFarland Jr. presiding.

The courtroom in the Simpson County Courthouse included a seldom-used, horseshoe-shaped balcony. Before integration, this balcony seating was the "Colored" section. For this trial, the balcony and every seat in the entire room was full.

The all-white jury sat to the right of the judge. No Black person had been selected, although the original jury list had the names of some Blacks on it. My lawyers, from the Lawyers' Committee for Civil Rights Under Law, were led by a young Black woman recently out of law school. Her name was Constance Iona Slaughter. She and the more experienced attorneys (Lawrence Ross, James Robertson, and James Abram) first objected to the all-white jury. In response, county officials were called to explain how they came up with the jury list. One supervisor said, "If I know someone personally, and I know he won't make a good juror, I don't put his name down." Aside from that statement, nothing more could be done about the jury. The judge ruled against all motions by the defense.

The next issue was that I still didn't know what law I was supposed to have violated. So my defense lawyer moved to dismiss the indictment or to continue the hearing only after the defendant was informed of a charge.

In response, District Attorney W. D. Adams insisted that he had never been asked by the defense for that information. My defense lawyers responded that they had indeed asked. Legal protocol was that they shouldn't have had to ask.

Finally, the DA revealed the charges. The state had accused me, Rev. John M. Perkins, of "willfully and unlawfully contributing to the delinquency of a minor under the age of sixteen years, whose name is Georgia Ann Quinn; willfully and unlawfully inducing and persuading said minor to enter and remain in the Simpson County Jail contrary to the instructions of Jimmy Griffiths, jailer of Simpson County. . . ."

In the affidavit attested to by the jailer, the name "Georgia Ann Quinn" was in a different handwriting than the rest of the document. Originally the word "unknown" had been written in and was still legible, though scratched over. Apparently, having decided that I should be charged with a crime, they had to find a specific child to whose delinquency I had contributed.

Still, they had to show some link between me and the girl's acts. The Mississippi justice system was accustomed to coping with such problems.

The prosecution's witness was Jimmy Griffiths, the jailer who had signed the original charges. Upon cross-examination, the jailer admitted he had locked the door on them all. How then, asked the astonished defense attorney, were they supposed to leave?

"Well," Griffiths replied, "we did lock the door behind them, but they were free to leave at any time. We almost begged them to leave." He further admitted that when the kids started pounding on the door, he opened a slot from his side to spray in some Mace. Griffiths never really tried to explain these and other curious events of that night.

Besides acting as jailer, Griffiths also frequently served as a courtroom deputy. The fact that he was a prosecution witness in the present trial did not bother the court officials; he remained in his usual place as a bailiff when not on the witness stand.

During one recess, Griffiths was seen standing in the jury area and chatting with one of the jurors. A defense lawyer noticed this violation of court procedure and objected. The objection drew a sharp rebuke from the judge: "You've just come into my courtroom a few minutes ago, and you're already telling me how to run things!"

The defense then asked for consultation in the judge's chambers, out of the hearing of the jury. Inside the chambers, they moved for a mistrial. The judge, after hearing Griffiths tell his version of the conversation with the juror, overruled the motion.

Judge McFarland appeared amazed that anyone should dare object to a situation in which a prosecution witness is also a court bailiff *and* hangs around the jury area. But he grudgingly agreed to rule that deputies and other law officers stay away from the jury for the rest of the trial.

However, the hearing in the judge's chambers revealed that the juror and Griffiths clearly knew each other, even though during the jury selection, each juror claimed in court that he did not personally know Griffiths. It would be difficult to pin this down on appeal since there was no transcript of the questioning of prospective jurors.

Next, eleven-year-old Georgia Ann Quinn was called by the prosecution to testify on how she came to be part of the group that visited the jail. The prosecution was never able to show that I had made any effort to persuade her to go to the jail or to remain there.

The trial went on for two days, longer than most trials of this kind. The whole business was beginning to get to me. While I was on the stand, prosecuting attorneys accused me of every kind of vileness. I began to despair. There was no way that I could refute their charges, not in this courtroom before this all-white jury. They were breaking me, and I knew it.

Finally, the judge pounded his gavel, calling a recess. I made my way back to a water fountain near the courtroom entrance and stood there a moment in misery. Then I walked out of the courtroom, alone. Other Blacks would have crowded around me had we been winning the case. But now, people didn't know what to say.

A little Black woman came up to me, face-to-face. She was perhaps seventy-five, dark-skinned, square-jawed. Looking me straight in the eyes, she said in a soft, commanding voice, "Stand up, son!"

That's all, just "Stand up, son!"

God must have sent her. She was just what I needed. I will never forget her face or those three words. Yes, I could stand up. I would stand up. Because I knew I wasn't standing alone! I wasn't standing only for myself.

I sucked in my stomach and threw back my shoulders. With new stamina in my heart, I walked back into that courtroom, ready for round two.

The trial went on. My defense lawyers attacked every statement of their charge. To be "contributing to the delinquency of a minor," they argued, you must first have a minor who is behaving in a delinquent way. That sounded sensible. But there was nothing in Miss Quinn's behavior at any time to establish her delinquency as defined by the statute.

The overwhelming evidence was that all these events resulted from the jailer's actions—not mine—since all of us would have come and gone peaceably and legally if we had been allowed to do so.

The maneuvering by the defense was to no avail. I was found guilty as charged, the jury requiring only a few minutes to reach the decision. For my "arrogance" in appealing the earlier sentence of $300 and three months, I was now sentenced to pay a fine of $400 and to spend four months in the county jail.

My defense attorneys immediately filed motions of appeal to the Mississippi Supreme Court. The appeal was duly considered some months later.

From the numerous defense points for appeal, one was granted as a reversible error: the issue of a state witness also serving as bailiff and conversing with a juror. This, of course, didn't address the real question of whether I contributed to the delinquency of a minor. It did place the burden on the lower court to either give me another trial or drop the charges.

In this situation, the best that my lawyers could do was a bit of horse trading. They had already filed a lawsuit against the county protesting the all-white jury. They still held this one card in their favor.

But since there was still an unresolved charge of disturbing the peace, a bargain was struck. I would plead guilty to the lesser charge of disturbing the peace and drop my lawsuit against the county. In court, the district attorney would then make a public statement that it was "not in the best interest of Simpson County" to bring me to trial again on the criminal delinquency charge.

Nobody won, and nobody lost. Justice, Mississippi style, had been served.

Yet, what turned out to be only a draw on paper in many ways was a real victory for the Black community of Mendenhall. Like the boycott, the Mendenhall trial helped to unify the Black community.

For the first time, our people saw a young Black woman lawyer—a Mississippi Black woman, at that—stand in Mendenhall's courtroom and argue a major case. That had never happened before in Simpson County.

They also saw a local Black person go into that courtroom, lose a case, and come out without going to jail. Our people saw that losing a case in the local court was no longer the end of the road. They saw us appeal all the way to the Mississippi Supreme Court.

They also saw that when the Supreme Court found out how rigged the administration of justice was at the local level, the highest court in the land sent the case back to the local court and told them to settle it right there, which they did. And our people saw that.

In a real sense, the local court lost the power to intimidate Blacks. And local Blacks won a great moral victory. The inspiration of that victory still motivates and liberates Mendenhall's Black community today.

# At the Gates
# of Justice

The law was not finished with us yet. Even before the Mendenhall trial began, twenty-three of us who had been arrested and beaten that brutal night in Brandon (the students arrested on Highway 49, several Voice of Calvary coworkers, and me) were all charged with various crimes.

I was charged with resisting arrest and so were some of the students, although it was never determined what acts constituted the offense or where the acts occurred. Several other charges—the most absurd being "carrying a concealed, deadly brick" (found in the back of the van)—were recorded.

Our lawyers petitioned to have our pending state criminal prosecution removed to the US District Court. A date was set for the district court to hear our petition for removal.

*Removal* is a term common to many civil rights cases throughout the country. Congress had passed laws protecting all marches, sit-ins, demonstrations, and other civil rights activities. This made it clear that when people were arrested for taking part in these kinds of activities, they would be tried in federal courts—and not be subject to the more prejudiced local courts.

To get around this, local authorities would arrest civil rights people on charges unrelated to the civil rights activities themselves. Therefore, they'd be tried in state courts. This was the reason the students were arrested in another county. The authorities were trying to nail us on charges that would keep us out of federal court. So our big legal struggle was to try to get our case removed from state court and into the federal court.

The first court to hear our case was the district court. The court's response was to narrow down the meaning of *removal* so that it would not apply to our case. Getting beaten in Brandon was dehumanizing. To see logical and rational minds being applied to legalizing the cause of racism was almost too much to take.

Our petition for removal was denied, and we were ordered to stand trial in the state courts. But our lawyers appealed our

## United States Justice System

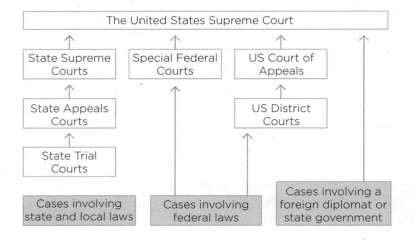

petition for removal to the US Court of Appeals for the Fifth Circuit. On January 14, 1972, a three-judge panel heard the appeal. By a two-to-one vote, our appeal was denied.

The two majority votes on the court were Judge Charles Clark and Judge James P. Coleman. Coleman was a former state attorney general and a former governor of the state of Mississippi. The one dissenting vote was cast by the chief judge of the court of appeals, Judge John R. Brown.

In these kinds of cases, judges defend their decisions by writing "opinions." The opinion written by the majority covers eleven pages in the court records. Judge Brown's dissent goes well over a hundred pages and is, in itself, an indictment of a legal system gone sour.

Judge Brown noted that there was no evidence at all for the charges against us. He also detailed the things that happened to us, and he called it what it was—*brutality*. He looked closely at the motives behind our arrests and the treatment of us, and he determined that hatred of civil rights workers, Black or white, was the true motive. He proved his points but was still outvoted.

In his dissent from the other justices, Judge Brown referred to a man and an event recorded in the book of Esther. After Haman was appointed chief counselor to the Persian king, Ahasuerus, he proposed a sweeping new law. All the members of the captive Jewish minority were to be branded as trouble-makers and destroyed. No one was to be spared.

Mordecai, uncle of Queen Esther, heard of the decree and was grieved. He tore his clothes in public mourning for his people. He "put on sackcloth and ashes, and went out into the midst of the city, wailing with a loud and bitter cry; he went up to the entrance of the king's gate, for no one might enter the king's gate clothed with sackcloth" (Esther 4:1–2

RSV). And there he remained as a public plea for the fate of his people.

Judge Brown presented this image of a people oppressed in an earlier period and drew a parallel with the plight of Black people in twentieth-century Mississippi. He wrote, "Rev. Perkins is like Mordecai at the Gate. His allegations and proof demand that we let him in."

As in the aftermath of the Mendenhall trial, once again a bit of legal horse trading provided our only way out of the Brandon arrests. Our lawyers had filed a lawsuit against the Mississippi Highway Patrol for their brutality. That lawsuit—though a perfectly fair and valid claim against the law officers—was dropped in return for the state's agreement not to prosecute the resisting arrest and other charges against the twenty-three defendants.

Again, there was no real vindication or legal victory. Not one of those doing the beating was ever punished. But after two years of legal maneuvering, my lawyers advised me to accept this compromise. It was not a satisfactory ending, just the benefit of not being put behind bars. And there's no telling what that might have meant for me.

I came away from the experience thinking that if sin can exist at every level of government and in every human institution, then the call to biblical justice must also be sounded in every corner of society by those who proclaim a God of justice as their Lord.

Judge Brown: we, like Mordecai, are still waiting at the gates of justice.

# Stronger
# Than Ever

First the hot, searing flash of open violence in early 1970. Then the dull, almost invisible progress of legal appeals. The memory of both simmered like pots on a stove's back burners. Every once in a while, someone stirred them up. Mostly, they just simmered.

On June 2, 1972—almost two years after my first arrest in Mendenhall—the final legal word was handed down by the full US Court of Appeals for the Fifth Circuit, followed by the last compromise between my lawyers and the prosecutors. Court or no court, we had plenty to do.

After being released from the Brandon jail in February 1970, Doug Huemmer, Curry Brown, and I spent a week getting our case together at our lawyer's home in Jackson. After seeing Dr. Smith, we went back to Mendenhall.

Mendenhall had a lot of new activities going on, but none of them could replace my Bible classes, youth meetings, and fellowship groups. These long-standing focuses of our work were nonnegotiable. I also spent one or two days a week speaking and organizing sessions for various economic cooperatives under the sponsorship of the Federation of Southern Cooperatives.

The Lord was helping me put things in the proper perspective. The sober lawyers and the laughing youngsters. The business problems and the prayer times. The new things and the old.

One Saturday in July 1970, the heat was so heavy it seemed to drip from the trees. I was sitting in my office in Mendenhall, getting things cleared up so I could go out to the ballpark and watch the kids play. That meant a lot to me. I love sports— and kids. Watching the kids play calmed my mind. And even though my original family was broken, I was always part of a family of kids who loved to play together.

Suddenly, I felt tired. Completely worn out. More tired than I had ever felt before. I went to my office, laid down, and fell asleep in the middle of the day. When I woke up, I didn't feel rested. Just wobbly, like I'd been sleeping for two or three days.

I don't remember how Sunday went. On Monday I convinced myself that I felt well enough to make the trip I'd planned to Mound Bayou, a small Black town in the Mississippi delta. So, I went.

I had helped organize some co-ops in Mound Bayou. On this trip, I observed their operations and talked with the managers. Afterward, a lady on the board of directors invited the board over for a nice dinner. I was so tired I could hardly sit up. I had terrible pain in my chest, so I ended up excusing myself to go lie down.

The next morning, I was rushed to the town's hospital—organized by Blacks for Blacks. The nurse found that my blood pressure was extremely high. I also had suffered a heart attack. I was immediately checked in and placed on bed rest. No traveling back to Mendenhall.

The days dragged by. One week. Two weeks. Maybe more. Slowly I began to feel stronger.

The doctors consulted with one another, comparing notes. Their conclusion: "Okay, we'll let you go home now, if you want to."

I really wanted to.

But back in Mendenhall, I began to feel sicker than ever. So I went back to the hospital in Mound Bayou, for three weeks this time. Then I returned to Mendenhall.

The fall of 1970 went by quietly. I kept a lighter schedule. Still, I started having stomach cramps.

In February 1971, a year after the Brandon beatings, I was finishing up a speaking engagement in Ann Arbor, Michigan. By the time I made it back to the plane after the meeting, I was doubled over with cramps.

Ulcers.

In the same Mound Bayou hospital as before, Dr. Harvey Saunders removed about two-thirds of my stomach. I spent three more weeks in the hospital and then took time for more rest and recovery at the home of friends in Mound Bayou. The health issues that began in February didn't get resolved until around the first of April.

Being hospitalized in Mound Bayou instead of in Mendenhall meant I was far enough away from the action to rest a little easier. The distance meant that I would be away from people coming in all the time and needing to talk. I also felt somewhat distant from the feeling that just down the road, I would encounter all kinds of unsettled problems and antagonisms. I guess God knew what I needed.

It's hard to explain what was going on with me. At no other time in my entire life—before or after accepting Christ—was having good health so crucial to my work, my thinking, and my well-being.

Going to Mound Bayou for all my medical treatments was absolutely vital if I was going to be able to meet the demands of our ministry's schedule. Mound Bayou was an all-Black community, and that kind of separate existence among Blacks was what I needed during those months of pain.

The emotional pain in my heart was just as real, just as raw, as the physical pain in my stomach. Everything pointed to the fact that justice was unlikely for a Black man in Mississippi, especially one who dared to stand up like a man.

It's hard to make this clear to white people, but a lot of Black people had come to this same conclusion—that there simply was no justice, no hope. Civil rights leaders didn't invent the injustices they talked about. They saw and felt oppression in a thousand ways. And the injustice was not just open brutality. It was ingrained in the system, in the fabric of Southern culture, as when economic and social structures form cages that neatly box the Black man in so that "nice" white folks can join the oppression without getting their hands dirty.

When you see and feel injustices in your soul, you can't stand still. White churches and white churchgoing businessmen seemed to accept this system and culture, even to the point of propping up a tradition that degraded and dehumanized Blacks. If you've never in your life seen a *true* Christian, then your vision is limited, focused in one direction. A lot of Blacks have taken that route. I don't mean those who talk about revolution. I mean Blacks who quietly build a life apart from God, the white God.

I was feeling the same pull to reject everything. My humanity, my whole self was telling me to reject everything that I had once worked for. Not to give up—oh, no! But to work for something different: to give up on whites and white Christians and to work only for me and mine. To work as a competitor rather than a colaborer.

Lying in the Mound Bayou Hospital bed, I pondered all the stages of our work at VOC. I thought about the suffering and bitterness unleashed by preaching what I thought was the gospel—the *whole* gospel. The *reconciling* gospel of Jesus Christ. Yet from the very start, our ministry in Mississippi faced threats and obstacles.

We had begun by preaching in the public schools and speaking in big tent meetings all over the county. After a number of converts had joined us, we began a Bible institute. It wasn't graduate seminary, but it taught young Black Christians to dig into the Bible and find out for themselves what it says.

I had tried to involve white teachers in our work, and a number of them were willing. Some drove all the way from Jackson to lecture for us. But Ku Klux Klan intimidation stopped that.

The civil rights movement that followed stirred up a blizzard of white emotions and Black expectations. I couldn't stand apart from it. I had to practice what I preached—a whole gospel for the whole man.

I became involved. My family became involved. VOC became involved. We did it because we knew *real* change would not come for Mendenhall's Blacks unless they gained their civil rights.

I headed up the voter registration drive in our county. But where would people register? We Blacks had no spare buildings on our side of the tracks. No whites in Simpson County would rent space to the federal marshals sent from Washington, DC, to help get Blacks registered. So we registered Blacks on the loading dock of the Post Office, the only federally owned property in town. I organized shuttle buses and vans for the registration effort.

We rode in fear. We registered in fear. And we voted in fear. Those Black voting lists were carved out in fear.

Because of my work for civil rights, my family was put in harm's way. Strange cars creeped past our house at night. Threatening phone calls jarred us awake in the wee hours of the morning. My wife and children lived in constant fear and anxiety—afraid for me and afraid for themselves.

I thought a lot about all this as I lay there in the hospital. Was it worth it? What was the point of it all? Was I accomplishing anything? Was I bringing the good news of the gospel to the people of Mendenhall? Or was I only creating more hatred and violence—and hurting more people, including my own children?

With genuine sadness, I pondered the gospel that I believed in with all my heart. The gospel that proclaims that in Christ there is no Black or white. I fully believed the gospel was powerful enough to shatter even the hatred in Mendenhall. But I had not seen it, especially in the churches.

On April 3, 1970—a month after my trial in Mendenhall—the state legislature repealed both the statutory prohibitions against racial integration and the criminal laws providing for racially segregated public facilities. Restaurants, schools, offices—even in Mississippi these places gradually began to integrate. But where was there an integrated church?

Tragically, but true, churchgoers in America are the slowest to change. So what did the future hold for integration in Mendenhall? In Mississippi? The land of Dixie? One of the South's most segregated states.

I thought deeply about the church and integration as I lay there. Day after day, I wondered whether the efforts were worth the aggravation. Dr. Saunders did a lot for me. So did Dr. Roberts. These two Black doctors saw me through my crisis. I was in a battle of the mind that could have destroyed me as much as any physical battle.

Images of hope began flickering anew in my heart and mind. I reflected on the positive impact we'd had on the young people of Mendenhall. Our first converts were now away at college, getting educated so they could return to teach others.

Spencer, my own son, had been one of the first to integrate Mendenhall's high school, one of a few Blacks among five hundred whites. He spent two terribly lonely years in that school. But he survived. In this family, in the VOC community, he had found the strength to survive. And already scores of others were now integrating schools—and surviving.

Slowly but surely, change was coming. The gospel was bringing changes. And I was a part of this change.

Other images also gave me hope. I knew there were whites who *did* care, whites who were supporting the work every month. White Christian doctors were treating me now and nursing me back to health. A white lawyer was preparing my legal case. White college graduates were working for VOC and earning less than one hundred dollars a month. Doug Huemmer and Ira Freshman, both whites, had endured the Brandon beatings and were arrested along with Black victims.

God was showing me something, telling me something. There were Blacks who had accepted our message, who had embraced the holistic application of the gospel. Who now realized their God-given dignity. Who now walked taller than they had before.

And there were whites who believed in justice, who lived love and shared themselves by joining our community.

In horror, I began to see how hate could destroy me—destroy me worse than any physical attack I could bring on those who had wronged me. I could try to fight back, as many of my brothers had done. But if I did, how would I be any different from the whites who hated Blacks?

Where would hate get me? Anyone can hate. This whole business of hating and hating in return keeps the vicious circle of racism going.

The Spirit of God worked on me as I lay in that bed. An image of Christ on the cross came to mind. It blotted out everything else I was thinking.

This Jesus knew what I had suffered. He understood, and He cared. Because He had experienced it all Himself.

This Jesus, this One who had brought good news directly from God in heaven, had lived what He preached. Yet He was arrested and falsely accused. Like me, He went through an unjust trial. He faced a lynch mob and was beaten. But even more than that, He was nailed to rough wooden planks and killed like a common criminal.

As Jesus hung on the cross, it must have seemed to Him that even God, His Father, had deserted Him. The suffering was so great that He cried out in agony. He was dying.

But when He looked at the mob that had lynched Him, He didn't hate those who crucified Him. He had compassion on them. Jesus loved them. He forgave them. And He prayed for

God to forgive them: "Father, forgive them; for they do not know what they are doing" (Luke 23:34 NRSV).

His enemies hated, but Jesus forgave. I couldn't get away from that.

The Spirit of God kept working on me and in me until I could say with Jesus, "I forgive them, too." I promised Him that I would return *good* for evil, not evil for evil. And He gave me the love and compassion I knew I would need to fulfill His command to love our enemies.

Because of Christ, God Himself met me at the point of my deepest need, healing my heart and mind with His love. I knew then what Paul meant in the book of Romans:

> Can anything separate us from the love Christ has for us? Can troubles or problems or sufferings? If we have no food or clothes, if we are in danger, or even if death comes—can any of these things separate us from Christ's love? . . . In all these things we have full victory through God who showed his love for us. Yes, I am sure that nothing can separate us from the love God has for us. Not death, not life, not angels, not ruling spirits, nothing now, nothing in the future, no powers, nothing above us, nothing below us, or anything else in the whole world will ever be able to separate us from the love of God that is in Christ Jesus our Lord. (8:35, 37–39 ICB)

The Spirit of God helped me to really believe what I had so often professed: that *only* through the love of Christ is there any hope for me or for those on whose behalf I had once worked so diligently. On that bed, God washed my hatred away and replaced it with a love for the white man in rural Mississippi. After that, God gave me the strength and motivation to rise up out of my bed and return to Mendenhall to spread a little more of His love around.

I felt strong again. Stronger than ever. What doesn't destroy me makes me stronger.

I know it's true.

It happened to me.

# The People of God

**S**omething else happened to me while in the hospital. God showed me that I couldn't do everything alone. I couldn't be a modern-day Moses, showing Blacks the way to the promised land all by myself.

I needed to build community spirit. I needed to learn to lean on people. We had to come together as colaborers for Christ. We had to become God's people—His church—if anything good was to happen in Mendenhall. We had to teach Blacks that the answer was not in following the white man's way of competition and power. We had to need each other, help each other, and love each other.

As I lay on my bed and thought and prayed over this, all the scars and hurts of the past seemed to fade away. I got another transfusion of God's hope.

I came out of that long stay in hospital in Mound Bayou not only determined to keep on with the work but also able to see more clearly the true heart of our work—it's *love*.

Groups have always seemed to me the best way to go about getting things done. Now I was seeing more clearly than ever how important it is for Christians to be the *people* of God and not just a collection of individual believers who gather weekly for worship on Sundays.

God's plan for our next steps were already been in motion. In June 1971, I saw one part materialize. Dolphus Weary, who we had worked with as a teenager and followed through college and graduate school, returned home to Mendenhall. He was able to take over the day-to-day responsibilities as executive director of Voice of Calvary. He managed the tutoring program and helped expand the Bible classes to five evenings a week. I was now able to work more on promoting new projects and fundraising.

There was plenty of need for additional funds. The expanded tutoring program was only one project in need of funds. The most notable project of 1972 was the completion of our new vocational workshop and gymnasium, which we had designed ourselves. We dedicated this all-purpose facility to the new generation of Black youth. We named it the R. A. Buckley Christian Youth Center in honor of a man, an old farmer, who was one of the greatest supporters of our young generation of leaders. Everyone at VOC pitched in to help with the building. We laid the concrete foundation ourselves. A contractor put up the steel framework. Then we constructed the cement-block walls. What was built in those months was more than just a building. Community was built. Years of conflicts, fears, and uncertainties had taken their toll, but the physical labor on a project of our own helped restore our sense of accomplishment and channeled bitterness into unity.

With the gym completed, we started work on another project—one that grew out of the devastating damage and deaths in 1969 from the great tornados in January and Hurricane Camille in August, a category five and the second most devastating storm to ever strike the United States. During these emergencies, Voice of Calvary helped provide food and clothing for the destitute. Our VOC program—including the co-ops and the immediate relief efforts—brought national attention and impressed national observers like *Jet* magazine and presidential assistant Robert Brown. Both came to Mississippi to observe the damage and the relief efforts.

After the tornado, the Community Education Extension used a research grant to survey the area and to examine not only the storm damage but also the overall health conditions of the people in the area. Vera Mae was a surveyor for Simpson County. The project continued from late 1969 to the time of the Brandon incident in February 1970. The survey uncovered alarming statistics and revealed what many local people already knew: poor health walked hand in hand with poverty throughout Simpson County.

Not only was there poor health in the Black community but we also needed to address poor medical care. The only white doctors who would treat Blacks had separate waiting rooms for Blacks and whites. On one side of the wall in the clinic was a carpeted, furnished waiting room designated for whites. Whites were treated immediately. Only after all white patients were treated would the doctor see Blacks from the other side of the wall. VOC envisioned a health center where every Black would be treated with respect and dignity.

In the fall of 1972, Erv and Joan Huston arrived to join the VOC staff. Erv had a degree from Bethany Seminary, and Joan was a registered nurse. They joined in the new effort of organizing a local cooperative health center, which extended through 1973. The idea was not simply to erect a free, mission-style health clinic but also to provide quality health care. This was the most expensive and challenging endeavor of our co-operative efforts.

The health center opened in 1973 with a couple of nurses and volunteer doctors. Finding our own full-time doctor was at the top of our prayer list. While prayers continued for a permanent doctor, the clinic project moved forward on faith. We installed a new X-ray machine worth $13,000. This technology would be a medical game changer for health diagnosis in our community. It was paid for through large and small donations from people in the community and around the country.

Friday, April 12, was to be a big day—the official dedication ceremony of the new clinic and X-ray machine. Our plans were interrupted by rain that began on Thursday night. By Friday morning, dark clouds covered the sky and torrential rains bore down on south-central Mississippi with no end in sight.

The Black section of Mendenhall was on the low edge of town. Dolphus Weary, sensing disaster, began mobilizing the Voice of Calvary staff to take all movable supplies and equipment to higher ground. Surely the rain would stop soon.

But the morning wore on without the rain slowing down. Nobody could remember when it had rained that hard before. The staff got busy again, this time moving people and furniture out of low-lying homes to higher ground. Our staff struggled through water already knee-deep by early afternoon.

Later, we heard that it rained a record-breaking fifteen inches in thirty hours. From where he stood on an embankment above the crest of the flood, Dolphus watched the angry waters push through the youth center. Through the church and tutorial school. Through the health center where our yet undedicated X-ray machine sat. A short distance away, the ravaging floodwaters tore away the fence around Dolphus's yard and pushed higher and deeper through the rooms of his house.

The dedication service had been set for four o'clock that Friday. Around two, Dolphus called me at the Jackson office and broke the news. Through blinding sheets of rain, I drove down to Mendenhall and joined Dolphus.

There wasn't much to say or much we could do. We stood there, watching the dreams of a lifetime—years of sweat, labor, laughter, and tears—dissolve inch by inch, minute by minute. Everything just floated away. God, forgive us for wondering why.

The havoc was beyond description. Most of the townspeople were shocked and paralyzed by their losses. Hope floated away with homes.

But God had given us at Voice of Calvary something that could not be lost. Something no flood could destroy. At this moment of devastation and ruin, we felt God restoring our courage and giving us the will to survive. We would face this challenge as we had other obstacles over the previous fourteen years. We would continue to identify the needs of the people and fill them in the name of Christ.

Our staff met together for prayer and "What next?" ideas. As we did, I reminded everyone that now more than ever the unity I had been calling for was absolutely necessary for the *whole* community.

Later that night, Black people met to share their despairs and to develop a strategy for survival. Again, prayer for unity was the key as I opened the meeting. With Dolphus Weary as chairman, the Community Disaster Committee was formed.

Within twenty-four hours, the committee had surveyed the total disaster area, even before the Red Cross arrived. The unity of effort crossed racial lines as the town's flood victims, mostly Black, called upon Mendenhall Mayor Ray Layton to represent their needs to the governor. Later, Layton said he believed he was appointed chairman over the county's disaster areas primarily because of the way the people of his own town unified to meet the challenge.

The slow cleanup began as the flood waters started to subside. The $8,500 damage to the X-ray equipment would eventually be addressed and the equipment restored.

But could the spirit of the community be restored? *Yes*. Despite our anguish, we saw that the Christian sense of community we had worked and prayed for had prevailed when everything else had washed away. The disaster had not taken with it our assurance of God's presence and protection.

Other answers to prayer were on the horizon. In Jackson, plans were being laid for a Bible institute focused on biblical training and Christian responsibility in society. I had been piecing together this program during our fifteen years of struggle. As I told the staff, we'd been busy doing a lot of things during these years, but we hadn't always managed to effectively communicate the nature and results of our work. Those on the outside, and even the volunteers who came for a few weeks of work, often didn't see beyond the bricks and the shovels. Communicating the vision and philosophy of our work was one of our biggest oversights.

In October 1974, the Jackson Bible Institute opened with four classes in a large old house we had recently purchased. We converted an old carriage house behind the main house into our offices. We established a small church and other community programs similar to those we had established years ago in Mendenhall. This was a place where young Blacks— and whites—could come together to discuss and agree about solutions for handling the issues of Christian community and to find significance in their own world. A philosophy of Christian community development was growing and flourishing.

In that same month, another breakthrough came. A young pediatrician, Dr. Eugene McCarty of Colorado Springs, Colorado, came to visit. He and his wife, Joanne, looked over our vacant health center and met the people in Mendenhall.

For several evenings, we talked far into the night. Then on Sunday, October 13, during the worship service in Mendenhall, the slender, soft-spoken doctor stood up and said, "My wife and I are convicted by what the Lord is doing here. We would like to become a part of your ministry, if you decide to have us."

There was shouting and crying during the service that day. Here was the answer to the prayers of people all over the county, prayers for a permanent doctor. But it was more than that. The coming of a doctor was a symbol of other things, too. Dr. McCarty was not just offering to come at a fraction of his former income on a short-term basis. He would become a part of our world.

Beyond that, this new development also further strengthened our call to Christian community. We were modeling authentic Christian fellowship. I remembered that my mother died of starvation when I was seven months old. I remembered my brother Clyde slipping away in my arms on the long drive to the hospital. I remembered the torture in the Brandon jail. I remembered how close I had come to death. Now there were these unbelievable opportunities. These giant steps for the Christian community made all the trials I had faced well worth the struggles.

Living out the gospel is indeed worth every sacrifice a person makes in this life. Christ living and working in us is what it means to be a Christian.

I *know* why my Lord saved me. And I *know* why He led me here. In a land where hatred once reigned unchallenged, I now see God, in His glory, carving out a pocket of love.

Where there was despair, there is now hope. Where there was oppression, there is now opportunity. Where there was defeat, there is now purpose. And where there was weakness, there is now strength—a strength that comes only from God.

> These things I suffer, but I am not ashamed, for I know whom I have believed, and am persuaded that He is able to keep that which I have committed to Him until that Day. (2 Tim. 1:12 MEV)

I face the future with courage and confidence born of faith in Jesus Christ alone. May His justice roll on.

# Reflection Questions

### Chapter 1: Clyde

Why did young John Perkins move to California? Give more than one reason.

### Chapter 2: Jap

What did John's cousins tease him about? Why was it hurtful?

### Chapter 3: Learning to Survive

What did a sharecropper's "making an arrangement" entail?

### Chapter 4: Challenging the System

How much was young John paid for his day's work at age twelve? Can you imagine how much that would be today? Can you explain why he uses the word *exploit*?

## Chapter 5: Who Needs Religion?

What was church life like where and when John grew up?

## Chapter 6: A Patch of Blue Sky

What did John mean by "a patch of blue sky" in his life?

## Chapter 7: God for a Black Man

What Bible character spoke strongly to John? Why?

## Chapter 8: Winners and Losers

Were you surprised that John desired to return to Mississippi? Why or why not?

## Chapter 9: A Hard Command

What caused Vera Mae to change her mind about moving to Mississippi?

## Chapter 10: Under the Skin

Can you explain what "separate but equal" means?

## Chapter 11: It's Nice to Have Friends

John found it was *not* hard to get Bibles donated for his ministry. But it *was* hard to get financial support from those same sources for attacking hunger and economic issues. Why do you think that was? Do you have an opinion about this?

## Chapter 12: The Whole Gospel

What does John mean by presenting the "whole gospel" to people? Can you give an example of what he means?

### Chapter 13: Taking a Stand

What are some reasons Blacks voting in Mississippi was so important at the time of this story?

### Chapter 14: The Key

In your own words, explain what a co-op is. Why did John feel co-ops were so necessary?

### Chapter 15: Disturbing the Peace

What was one or more procedure that the jailers did improperly during the arrest of John and his group?

### Chapter 16: Green Power

What time of year did the boycott occur, and why did that matter?

### Chapter 17: Ambush

The jail experience in this chapter is a hard story to read. What are your reactions to what happened?

### Chapter 18: Beyond Brandon

Why were Curry and Doug kicked out of a church? What are your thoughts about that?

### Chapter 19: Mississippi Justice

Who talked to John outside the courtroom? Why was that so important?

### Chapter 20: At the Gates of Justice

Who did Judge Brown compare John to in the Bible? Why?

## Chapter 21: Stronger Than Ever

How did John become strong again?

## Chapter 22: The People of God

How did the hurricane, flood, and tornado impact the Voice of Calvary work? What good came from these disasters?

# Reflection Discussions

1. How do racial issues in this book compare to racial issues in America today?

2. Do you see any parallels between John Perkins's world and our world today?

3. What has changed? What has not?

4. Compare and contrast the civil rights movement and the Black Lives Matter movement.

**John M. Perkins** is cofounder of the Christian Community Development Association and director of the John & Vera Mae Perkins Foundation in Jackson, Mississippi. He is the author of many books, including *Dream with Me* and *Let Justice Roll Down*, named by *Christianity Today* as one of the top fifty books that have shaped evangelicals.

**Priscilla Perkins** founded Harambee Preparatory School, specializes in the social foundations of education and cognitive development of children, and has experience in family law and legal research. Spending her whole life in ministry as a preacher's kid (the seventh child of John Perkins), Priscilla has important stories to tell. She is currently copresident of the John & Vera Mae Perkins Foundation.

# JOHN & VERA MAE PERKINS FOUNDATION

Head to **jvmpf.org** to learn more about the **John & Vera Mae Perkins Foundation** and how you can get involved, order books, and donate.